MELBOURNE'S MARVELLOUS TRAMS

UNSW PRESS

Melbourne & Metropolitan Tramways Board

Please step inside

RIDING ON FOOTBOARD PROHIBITED
PENALTY UP TO $50

DALE BUDD
RANDALL WILSON

CONTENTS

RAY MARSH

Collins Street Melbourne Victoria.

ACKNOWLEDGEMENTS

A UNSW Press book

Published by
University of New South Wales Press Ltd
The University of New South Wales
Sydney 2052 Australia

© D. Budd and R. Wilson

First published in 1998
Reprinted in 1998

National Library of Australia
Cataloguing-in-Publication entry:

Budd, Dale.

Melbourne's marvellous trams.

ISBN 0 86840 504 3.

1. Trams—Victoria—Melbourne. 2. Trams—Victoria—Melbourne—History. 3. Trams—Victoria—Melbourne—Pictorial works. 4. Tramways—Victoria—Melbourne. 5. Tramways—Victoria—Melbourne—History. 6 Tramways—Victoria—Melbourne—Pictorial works. 7. Tramways—Accidents—Victoria—Melbourne.
I. Wilson, Randall, 1951-.
II. Title.

388.46099451

Design: Dana Lundmark and Di Quick
Printer: Kyodo Printing, Singapore

The authors gratefully acknowledge the generous assistance of more than 40 individuals and organisations who, by making available photographs, paintings and numerous items of memorabilia, made this book possible.

The authors also thank the following people who lent their support in a variety of ways: David Jones, for his expert cartography and drawings of trams; David Brown, David Burke, Brian Carter, Louis de Vries, Andrew Foy, Graham Jones, Colin Kemp, Robert Lilburn, Mike McLeod, Jeff Moreau, Bill Parkinson, John Phillips, Cathy Quealy, Fred Saxon, Ron Scholten, Rod Smith, Shirlene Standish (Gas and Fuel Corporation), Michael Venn, Van Wilkins, Ross Willson, Richard Youl and Robert Young.

The permission of the Chartered Institute of Transport in Australia Inc. to reproduce the article 'Moving People' is gratefully acknowledged.

FURTHER READING

Melbourne's cable trams and the routes on which they ran:

John D Keating, *Mind the Curve! A History Of The Cable Trams,* Transit Australia Publishing, Sydney, 1996.
ISBN 0 909459 19 3

Jack Cranston, *The Melbourne Cable Trams 1885 to 1940,* Craftsman Publishing, Melbourne, 1988.
ISBN 0 9587833 7 3

Melbourne's electric trams from 1889 to the present:

Norman Cross, Dale Budd and Randall Wilson, *Destination City,* Transit Australia Publishing, Sydney, 1993.
ISBN 0 909459 17 7

Recent Melbourne's tramway system:

David R Keenan, *Melbourne Tramways,* Transit Press, Sydney, 1985.
ISBN 0 909338 04 3

PTCV

▲ A cable tram gripman pauses for a photograph during shunting movements at the northern terminus of Nicholson Street, North Fitzroy.

PREVIOUS PAGE In the years when horse-drawn vehicles were synonymous with road transport, the cable tram symbolised cleanliness and efficiency. In this Edwardian scene in Collins Street, affluent city shoppers and other pedestrians wait for a cable tram to pass en route to middle class North Fitzroy.

FOREWORD

BY KEITH DUNSTAN

Melbourne is a sensitive place. A few years back we began wondering about the exact location of the Melburnian soul. Some thought it had to be under the clocks of Flinders Street Station. Others thought, oh no, it would be somewhere near the goal posts of the Melbourne Cricket Ground. On the other hand there was a strong feeling that the soul surely had to be under the Shrine of Remembrance built in memory of the diggers who lost their lives in various wars. There was Chloe too, the bashful nude in Young & Jackson's Hotel. She was a symbol of Melbourne.

It was in the early 1970s that we suddenly realised the truth; the soul of Melbourne was a moving thing. Our soul was in the green and gold trams. They were the last of their kind in the whole nation and other cities were pleading to purchase them. Places such as Hong Kong, Portland in Oregon and even the celebrated tram city, San Francisco, wanted some of our trams. Indeed the green and golds had a mystic wonder as they trundled their way towards St Kilda Junction, climbed the heights towards Burwood or pushed their way west to Footscray.

It was not always thus. During the 1960s there was a concentrated effort to get rid of this outdated 'virtually medieval' form of transport. They interfered with the god motor car. They could delay a man five minutes, even ten, in his vital rush to his office chair. They were the very devil to pass in High Street, Preston, virtually impossible in Sydney Road, Brunswick, and the Toorak millionaires literally fumed behind the wheels of their Mercedes in Toorak Village.

Leading writers in newspapers unanimously agreed that trams had to go. Look at other cities, they said: Sydney, Adelaide, Brisbane, Perth. They were all switching to the splendidly mobile buses. Buses did not take up the middle of the road; they pulled into the kerb.

The redoubtable Major General Sir Robert Risson, then Chairman of the Melbourne and Metropolitan Tramways Board, fought a rearguard action. He pointed out that trams lasted 50 years longer than buses, they were more efficient, at peak hour, they could shift four times the number in half the time, and, even more telling, they were environmentally pure. They did not pump out the toxic filth of cars and buses. So Sir Robert the old soldier won his Dunkirk.

The official recognition that the tram was pure Melbourne and a tourist symbol did not come until 1994. The government introduced the City Circle route — a tram every 10 minutes from 10 am to 6 pm would run both ways around the city along Flinders, Spencer, La Trobe and Spring Streets. They used classic W class trams, the oldest dating from 1936. They all had over a million miles on the clock. I remembered the W class well indeed; they took me to school every day. They were as draughty as a tree, they had wooden seats designed to straighten even the most bent backs, and they had running boards on which the more daring of us rode when the tram inside was sardine-packed.

However, the City Circle Ws were remodelled for the tourist trade. Now you will find they have padded seats, sliding doors to keep out the Antarctic southerlies, and what has been a deep shock to the purists, they have been painted burgundy instead of the traditional green and gold. But never mind, they still make the same old hysterical scream as they grind metal on taking a curve.

In Melbourne for many years I wrote a daily column, and I discovered very early that there was a huge band of tram enthusiasts. They were a force with which to be reckoned. One dared not to make a mistake. Their technical knowledge was beyond belief. If one incorrectly named a model, foolishly identified a tram part in an improper manner, or even misjuggled a tram timetable, there was an avalanche of correspondence.

I discovered that these people not only loved trams, they loved everything about them. There was even a group that went about recording tram noises. There is a curious thumping the older Ws make when they stop. It sounds as if they need a triple by-pass, but they are restoring their energies to move on. This is particularly recordable. So while non-tram people may like to play rock or Beethoven when they are feeling weary, a tram lover will restore his calm and wellbeing by playing back tram noises.

Such people are Dale Budd and Randall Wilson. Dale has a vast technical knowledge of both trams and trains. Randall, if it is possible, has trams in his blood. He was born within ear-shot of Melbourne's trams. If you come from Melbourne, that is not difficult. In our house you could hear the first tram go past at precisely 5.35am. And that beat the hell out of the first cuckoo or even the first magpie.

INTRODUCTION

What is it about trams that attracts our interest? To some, particularly car drivers in busy streets, they are unwelcome. To others, they are strictly utilitarian — a means of getting to work and home again, and not a means of travel for pleasure.

But for many, trams have an intangible appeal. In a rapidly changing world, trams on their fixed and well-defined routes are a symbol of reliability. If you wait at a tram stop, a tram will surely come. And when it comes, you will probably be able to squeeze on, no matter how crowded it is. Those who wait at bus stops have no confidence in either of these things. The much-vaunted 'flexibility' of buses means that the wretched rubber-tyred vehicle has probably gone some other way.

Steam trains have an appeal for many people. A steam locomotive with its sounds and smells and its visible and audible evidence of effort seems as close to being human as any machine can be. But steam engines were often sooty and dirty. And apart from those preserved by museums, they have gone. In contrast, trams are here and now. They represent one of the few technologies which was invented in the 19th century and is surviving into the 21st. Basic elements of the technology have not changed, allowing trams built in the 1890s and which have been maintained as heritage items, to operate occasionally on the networks of today.

The first successful electric tram system was built by Frank J Sprague and installed in Richmond, Virginia, USA in 1887. After a few months of teething troubles, the success of the electric trams was quickly recognised, leading to their very rapid adoption in other cities. By the end of 1889 there were no less than 154 electric tram systems running in the USA. These systems were either new, or they replaced inefficient horse-drawn systems or successful but costly cable tram networks. The name Frank Sprague has largely been forgotten, but among the other accomplishments of this capable engineer was the development of high speed lifts with reliable control systems, which enabled the construction of multi-storey buildings.

The new electric tram technology spread rapidly to other countries including Australia, where the first electric tram line opened in Melbourne in 1889. Sydney tested electric trams in 1890, and other Australian cities soon followed.

The rapid spread of trams led to a remarkable degree of uniformity. Electricity supplied at 600 volts direct current became a world standard that is still in use today, albeit with an increase to 750 volts on newer systems. A very large number of systems adopted the standard railway gauge of 4′8½″ inches, later 1435mm. In Australia uniformity was demonstrated by the fact that Brisbane, Sydney and Melbourne all had standard gauge tramways, although the respective states had three different gauges for their railway networks.

As a leading supplier of urban public transport, the tram flourished until the rise of the motor car

RAY MARSH

in the 1920s began to revolutionise travel patterns. With declining patronage, soon accelerated by the Depression, buses were a lower-cost alternative for many smaller systems — and for some larger ones.

Petrol rationing during the Second World War brought a respite before public transport, including trams, renewed its battle against the motor car.

Many cities in Europe, and a few elsewhere, retained their trams. (The reasons for Melbourne keeping its trams are discussed later in this book.) Eventually it was realised that the motor car with its insatiable appetite for road space is detrimental to livable, attractive cities.

After years of relegation to inferior status, the desirable features of trams were recognised anew. Of all vehicles, trams are best suited to serve city centres, providing access without intrusion. Tram technology has been developed, offering smoother and quieter vehicles, with stylish appearance and passenger comfort.

Cities all over the world which had abandoned trams began to plan and implement their return: London, Paris and Los Angeles are but three of the many cities with new tram systems. One hundred years after electric trams were invented, they are achieving new levels of popularity.

So it is a blend of characteristics which makes trams attractive. They are dependable for their passengers, socially beneficial and environmentally desirable. They combine much that is good from the past, with features essential to the survival and prosperity of our cities in the 21st century. They are a welcome part of our lives.

▲ With dust from the peak traffic period still in the air, mid-morning sunshine bathes the eastern end of Collins Street.

◀ A near-empty tram is reflected momemtarily in the calm waters of the Yarra River as it crosses Hawthorn Bridge.

ERA OF THE CABLE TRAMS

Like San Francisco and Chicago, Melbourne was one of the great, fast-growing cities of the late 19th century. Yet little remains today of Melbourne's cable tram network which exceeded San Francisco's in size and was one of the most efficient and technically advanced in the world.

Designed and built between 1885 and 1891 essentially as a single entity, Melbourne's cable tram system epitomised sophistication and excellence in city transport at the time of its construction. On completion the system comprised nearly 75 km of double track serving 17 routes.

For most of its life, the system was operated by the Melbourne Tramway and Omnibus Company until it passed into government ownership in 1916. At that time the Company was operating 480 grip cars (known as 'dummies'), 460 standard four-wheel trailer cars and 56 larger bogie trailers.

From the early 1920s, it became clear that the cable system could not meet the transport requirements of the steadily expanding city. Sixteen years after closure of the city's first cable line, Melbourne's last cable tram ran on 26 October 1940, decades before the historical significance of the system would be appreciated by governments or many of the city's residents.

▲ The first trams in some Melbourne suburbs were drawn by horses. Most of these lines, which operated in Coburg, Hawthorn, Kew, Royal Park, Fairfield, Caulfield and Beaumaris, were later absorbed into the electric tram network. In a scene probably typical of this period, horses struggle to pull an overloaded car towards the terminus of the Beaumaris horse tramway.

◀ 'A glimpse of Collins Street …': Cable trams bound for Port Melbourne and North Fitzroy pass near the site of today's city square.

8

▶ Swanston Street and St Kilda Road were the busiest of Melbourne's cable tram lines, servicing the south-eastern suburbs of Toorak, Windsor and Prahran. One hundred years ago, a lightly loaded cable tram heads towards Princes Bridge and the system's most southerly destination of Brighton Road, having negotiated its way through a multitude of delivery wagons and carts in the city's commercial heart.

Swanstone St., Melbourne

▼ Face of a maturing city: Well-dressed ladies have a panoramic view from the front of the dummy as they travel down Collins Street past the Town Hall.

Collins Street, Melbourne

◀ For over 100 years trams have played their part in moving people to and from sporting events ranging from football and cricket to the Olympic Games and Grand Prix motor racing. In the 1920s trams in Bridge Road collect punters returning from the Richmond Pony Racecourse.

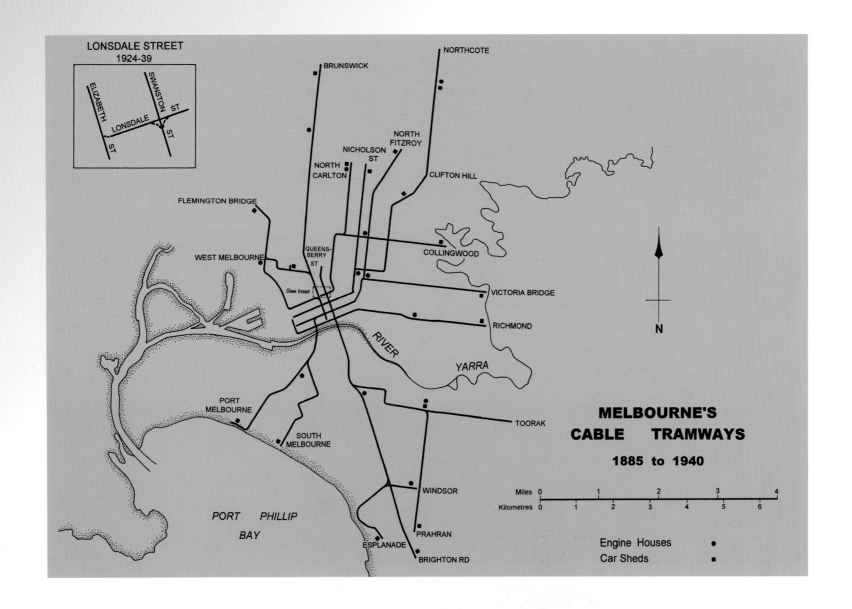

LONSDALE STREET
1924-39

ELIZABETH ST
SWANSTON ST
LONSDALE ST

NORTHCOTE

BRUNSWICK

NORTH
FITZROY

NICHOLSON
ST

NORTH
CARLTON

CLIFTON HILL

FLEMINGTON BRIDGE

COLLINGWOOD

QUEENS-
BERRY
ST

WEST MELBOURNE

See Inset

VICTORIA BRIDGE

RIVER

RICHMOND

YARRA

N

PORT
MELBOURNE

TOORAK

SOUTH
MELBOURNE

**MELBOURNE'S
CABLE   TRAMWAYS**

1885 to 1940

WINDSOR

Miles   0   1   2   3   4
Kilometres 0   1   2   3   4   5   6

PRAHRAN

PORT   PHILLIP

BAY

ESPLANADE

BRIGHTON RD

Engine Houses   ●
Car Sheds   ■

PTCV

JACK CRANSTON COLLECTION

△ Swanston Street in the 1920s: Saturday morning office workers mingle with shoppers as they make their way to city tram stops and south to Flinders Street Station.

△ Melbourne's first cable tram route, built in 1885, connected the city with the inner working class suburb of Richmond some 5.8 km east of the city.

With Hosie's Hotel on its left, a Richmond-bound tram approaches Elizabeth Street before ascending the grade to the busy junction with Swanston Street.

ROSE POSTCARD, VIC SOLOMONS COLLECTION

▶ On a warm afternoon in the early 1920s, a South Melbourne cable tram passes along Bridport Street, Albert Park.

Conductors on cable trams used a bell-punch system for fare collection. Passengers were not issued with tickets but for each fare collected the conductor punched one of a series of numbered squares on one of several coloured 'trip slips' attached to his jacket. Each time the punch was used it sounded a bell, which assured the passenger that his fare had not been pocketed by the conductor. The fares represented by the confetti-like pieces contained in each bell punch were later compared with the money taken by each conductor to ensure the two matched.

Use of the bell punch suggests that the Melbourne Tramway and Omnibus Company was more concerned with the dishonesty of conductors than the dishonesty of passengers.

As Melbourne's cable trams comprised two units — a grip car (or dummy) which towed a saloon car — the order of each had to be reversed at the terminus of each route often with the assistance of passengers. This mid-1920s scene shows shunting movements under way at the Toorak terminus in Toorak Road.

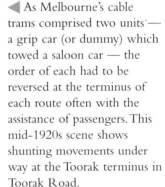

◀ The signing of the Armistice on 11 November 1918 was celebrated through-out the British Empire by the decoration of buildings and public places. Public transport had some special roles during the war, being used first to promote recruitment and later to help celebrate the victory.

PTCV

Bird's Eye View, Melbourne

VIC SOLOMONS COLLECTION

◀ Faithfully restored by tramways staff of the Preston Workshops, Melbourne's first cable tram ran almost continuously for 55 years. It is now on display at the Scienceworks science museum in the inner south western suburb of Spotswood.

▲ Successive decades of prosperity in the latter half of the 19th century, culminating in the speculative extrava-gance of Marvellous Melbourne in the 1880s, gave the city a heritage of fine public buildings. In this scene dating from the 1890s, an in-bound cable tram glides past the colony's Treasury towards the intersection of Spring and Collins Streets.

PTCV

THE EARLY ELECTRIC YEARS

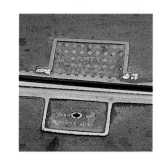

Melbourne's first electric tram ran in 1889, on a pioneering line from Box Hill to Doncaster. This short-lived operation ceased in 1896, and it was another 10 years before electric traction returned in the form of the much more substantial service of the Victorian Railways from St Kilda to Brighton Beach. In the same year privately owned lines opened from Flemington Bridge to Essendon and Maribyrnong River. Both of these were feeder services, linking respectively with steam trains at St Kilda and cable trams at Flemington Bridge. Over the next decade other electric lines were built as feeders to the cable network, operated by trusts formed by local councils.

A program of reform between 1916 and 1922 saw the whole network, cable and electric, brought under unified control, with the exception of the Victorian Railways lines. By then these lines consisted of two routes, from St Kilda to Brighton Beach and from Sandringham to Black Rock.

The newly-formed Melbourne and Metropolitan Tramways Board launched a program of conversion of the cable system to electric traction, and construction of new electric lines. This program was not effectively completed until 1956, which was also the year in which the last of the famous W series trams was placed in service.

▲ Trams were elaborately decorated for special occasions, such as the openings of new lines, anniversaries or other patriotic events. This tram is about to leave Malvern Depot, decorated for the Coronation of King George V in 1911.

At the turn of the 20th century, electric trams were without doubt the finest vehicles on the roads. Before the days of traffic congestion, they were objects of universal admiration. This picture shows No 4 of the Prahran and Malvern Tramways Trust in Glenferrie Road, either on a trial run or on opening day on 30 May 1910. The ornamental poles in the centre of the road, supporting the overhead wiring for the trams, were an early victim of road improvements. They were removed from Glenferrie Road in 1915, although they remain in busy locations such as Fitzroy Street, St Kilda, to this day.

▲ Hardly a motor vehicle in sight, and even a scarcity of horse-drawn conveyances, as a tram sets out along Dandenong Road from the corner of Chapel Street, bound from Windsor to Wattletree Road, Malvern. This quiet scene dates from the later years of the First World War.

▼ In the days before road transport was capable of carrying substantial loads, several specially converted trams performed this task. Freight Car No 2A has since been restored to near original condition (see page 55).

▶ The designers of Melbourne's first electric tram must have had optimistic views about the city's climate – or about the willingness of travellers to brave the elements. This is 14 October 1889, opening day of Melbourne's, and Australia's, first electric tramway line, from Box Hill to Doncaster. This tram and one other operated for some seven years on this pioneering line, which ran through open countryside. Tram design was to evolve rapidly over this period, providing much greater comfort for passengers, and greater speed and reliability.

▶ With growth in the number of motor vehicles, parking in Collins Street seems to have been a problem as early as the 1920s. While a number of historic buildings in this section of Collins Street were demolished in the post-war period, many others remain, thus preserving the 19th century character of this part of the city.

▲13 November 1913: Opening day for the Prahran and Malvern Tramways Trust's line to Elsternwick. There is an air of excitement as a procession of trams makes its way along Glenhuntly Road.

▶ The usefulness of trams for advertising was recognised almost from the beginning. This open-sided tram, normally used for cleaning the track and other utilitarian duties, was decked out during the First World War to promote recruitment.

WHERE CITY AND COUNTRY MEET.—Sheep on the road to the New-market yards held up traffic yesterday. Their drovers did not hold a stop-work meeting, as they had threatened to do.

◄ Early days on the Essendon lines: A North Melbourne Electric Tramways and Lighting Company tram is delayed in Racecourse Road, Newmarket, by a flock of sheep on their way to the Newmarket saleyards in the 1920s. Such scenes were repeated until the 1960s when a bridge was built across the road.

◄ Down through the years, the completion of new tramway lines has often been celebrated by formal ceremonies and an element of fanfare. On 1 April 1920, officials of the Fitzroy, Northcote and Preston Tramways Trust join with locals for the departure of the first tram to East Preston.

▼ Until 1957 all-night trams ran on most routes, providing a reliable service for those needing to travel between midnight and dawn. As travellers turned to cars or taxis, a decline in patronage led to the end of the all-night trips, which were mostly provided by older and smaller trams converted for driver-only operation. This elderly four-wheeler, built in the early 1920s, is about to begin a nocturnal run to West Maribyrnong from the city terminus at Elizabeth and Flinders streets.

CITY & ENVIRONS

Melbourne's distinctive grid-like pattern of wide streets interspersed with tree-lined boulevards owes much to the vision of influential figures such as its first Lieutenant Governor, Charles Joseph La Trobe who laid out the city's parks and gardens, and its first Surveyor General, Robert Hoddle who planned the city's major thoroughfares. Hoddle's legacy was a city remarkably well suited to 20th century transport, at least until the large-scale ownership and use of private cars became evident in the 1960s.

◄ For over 40 years, centre poles graced William Street until traffic conditions necessitated their replacement by conventional wiring with kerbside poles. In this 1972 scene, a tram emerges from shadows to slow down at the intersection of William and Bourke Streets.

▼ Homeward-bound office workers with Coburg and Essendon trams in their sights as they hurry towards the terminus of the Elizabeth Street lines in the mid-1970s. Overlooking the scene is the rundown facade of Flinders Street Station, since restored to its original appearance.

DAVID MACARTNEY

CITY NOLAN ST
ARTS CENTRE
DOMAIN &
ST KILDA RDS CNR
ST KILDA BEACH
CITY

BRIAN ANDREWS

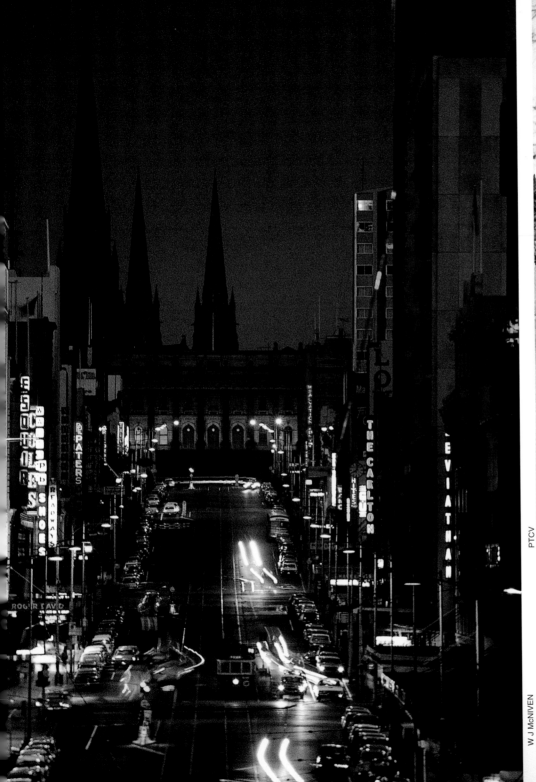

W J McNIVEN

PTCV

◀ With the evening peak period over, a solitary W series tram pauses at the intersection of Bourke and Swanston streets in the early 1970s. The tram will shortly proceed past the retailing stores of Myers and Coles, through the section later to be known as the Bourke Street Mall.

▲ The Yarra River, once one of Melbourne's less attractive waterways, has returned to prominence in recent years with the development of major office, retail and hotel accommodation at Southbank.

CITY CIRCLE

The City Circle, completed in April 1994, enables trams to travel in both directions around the central district. The service is free. Information on points of interest and places to visit is provided on board the trams.

DALE BUDD

WILLIAM F SCOTT

▲ When the City Circle route was established, there was general agreement that the service should be operated by W series trams. Although a break with tradition, the burgundy-red colour scheme, with gold and cream trim and a dark green roof clearly identifies the ten City Circle trams from the rest of the fleet.

RANDALL WILSON

▲ Located opposite Parliament House is the Princess Theatre, renowned for its Second French Empire architecture and roll-back ventilating roof.

◀ A City Circle tram pauses at the corner of Bourke and Spring streets, a convenient stepping-off point for the elegant Windsor Hotel or Parliament House.

▶ Little is recognisable today of this scene which dates from the late 1960s. Collins Book Depot and the Travellers Hotel have made way for the eastern entrance to Melbourne Central station. Overshadowed by the Melbourne Central complex is Jensen House, the last office building constructed in the city before the outbreak of the Second World War.

▲ Pedestrians amble through the historic Fitzroy Gardens, one of several picturesque locations served by trams operating along Flinders Street.

GIVE WAY TO TRAMS

The Gothic architecture of Australia's largest church, St Patrick's Cathedral, dwarfs tram No 644 as it accelerates down Gisborne Street, East Melbourne.

▼ Two Z series trams in their original orange colour scheme pass at the intersection of Flinders and William streets, an area overshadowed by the viaduct completed in 1891 to connect the city's two main railway stations.

In early 1996 a new terminus was opened at Melbourne University, incorporating a third track in the middle of the road. Three freshly painted W series trams manoeuvre through the new track layout soon after its completion.

DALE BUDD

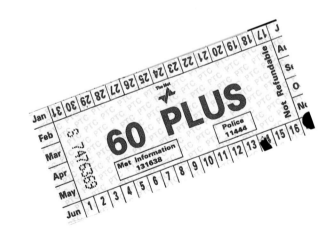

RAY MARSH

Light of the world: The awe-inspiring sight of St Paul's Cathedral floodlit by night greets mid-evening tram travellers in Swanston Street.

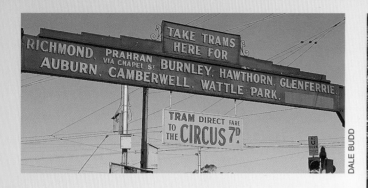

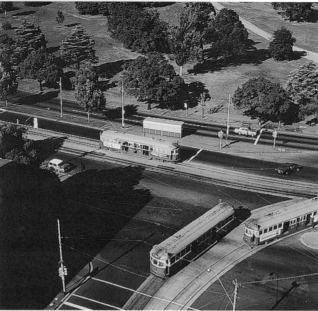

◀ The green and cream colour scheme applied to Melbourne's trams was introduced in 1925 on buses formerly operated along St Kilda Road by the Melbourne and Metropolitan Tramways Board. These colours were chosen to blend with the tree-lined thoroughfare. In hindsight, the choice has stood the test of time, as shown by this high-level view of trams at the junction of Park Street, South Melbourne, and St Kilda Road.

▶ Construction of a tunnel beneath St Kilda Road as part of the Arts Centre project in the 1970s resulted in significant changes to the streets of inner South Melbourne. One such change involved removal of the intersection of St Kilda Road and City Road to make way for the impressive theatre complex now situated on Southbank. In this late 1960s scene, a South Melbourne tram swings into St Kilda Road from City Road, before crossing Princes Bridge en route to the city.

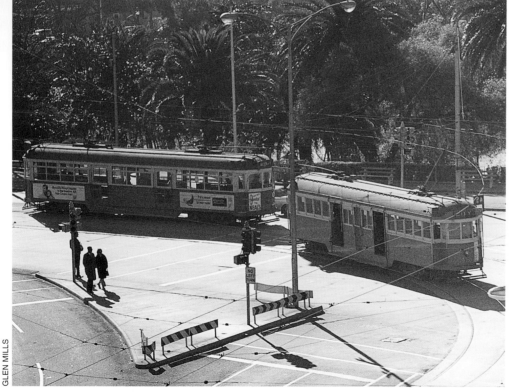

▲ Leaving behind the congestion of the city, the tram painted by Clifton Pugh arrives at the intersection of Gisborne Street and Victoria Parade, an area known to 19th century Melburnians as Eastern Hill. The tram will shortly cross Victoria Parade, one of the city's busiest tramway junctions, before entering Brunswick Street en route to the northern suburb of West Preston.

◀ Winter evening in Collins Street: Passengers walk briskly in the direction of Spencer Street Station as crews hurry to shunt their trams in the fading light.

W J McNIVEN

◀ The city by night: The monumental and highly decorative colonnade of Parliament House looms over an in-bound tram as it turns from Spring Street into Bourke Street.

W J McNIVEN

WHY MELBOURNE KEPT ITS TRAMS

At the beginning of 1950, thirteen Australian cities had tram systems: Brisbane, Sydney, Newcastle, Melbourne, Geelong, Ballarat, Bendigo, Adelaide, Perth, Fremantle, Kalgoorlie, Hobart and Launceston. Twenty-five years later, only Melbourne retained a large network. All the others had gone, except for a single line in Adelaide, running mainly on off-street track from the city to Glenelg. Small remnants remain in use in Ballarat and Bendigo for tourist or heritage services.

What were the factors which led to the widespread abandonment of tram operations? Why did they not apply in Melbourne?

It is interesting to examine the situation which applied in Sydney, a city of similar size to Melbourne. At the beginning of the 1950s, Sydney's tram network was equivalent in route length to that of Melbourne, although it carried more passengers and had a much larger fleet of trams.

▲ Melbourne's streets are generally wider than those of Sydney, and the operation of trams on inner suburban boulevards such as Royal Parade, Parkville, presents few problems.

▼ A busy morning in Sydney in the mid-1920s. Trams wait to load passengers at Central Station for the trip to the central city area. Modern trams returned to this part of Sydney in 1997.

VIC SOLOMONS COLLECTION

▶ Paris was unusual among European cities in abandoning trams in the 1930s, largely in favour of underground Metro rather than buses. As in many other cities, trams have returned to Paris. This stylish vehicle is in the northern suburb of St Denis.

◀ Ballarat is typical of the cities which were too small to sustain tram systems. Two trams are seen en route from Mount Pleasant shortly before the end of operations in 1971. Happily, a short section of track alongside Lake Wendouree is still used for a heritage service.

A succession of transport authorities in Sydney had dithered with plans to replace trams with buses from the early 1930s until the decision was finally taken in 1953. Many of the trams in Sydney were very old, dating from before the First World War. Their cross-bench or 'toast-rack' design, while giving high seating capacity, was seen as outdated. The tracks were old and in poor condition, and had suffered from deferred maintenance during the Second World War.

The cost of renewing and updating the system was daunting. The administration became obsessed with the lower operating costs of buses. Purchase of a fleet of modern buses, suitable for one-person operation, could sweep away the cost burdens of the tram network.

A succession of consultants from overseas recommended replacement of the trams, based on trends in Britain and North America. There were many cities whose tram systems had similar characteristics, particularly obsolete equipment, and where replacement by buses appeared the easy way out.

Other factors in Sydney, including the sharp decline in public transport patronage following the Second World War, accompanied a strong rise in motor vehicle ownership. It was foreseen that the reduced demand for public transport could be met by buses. The roads and motoring lobbies decried trams, which were thought to cause congestion in narrow city streets. The media supported the replacement of trams in the interest of modernity.

Queen Street, Brisbane, looks little different from the centre of Melbourne in this 1968 scene. Less than a year later the trams had gone, but proposals have been made for their return to the northern capital.

Of all the world's cities, Los Angeles has become most closely identified with freeways and the motor car, but for some years a revival of public transport has been under way. A modern tram loops its way through the streets of Long Beach before heading north to the centre of Los Angeles. This route, abandoned in 1961, was the first to have rail services restored in 1990.

Some of these arguments had validity. For smaller cities the reality of the decline in demand for public transport and the lower costs of buses meant that they were the more appropriate option. However, the decision makers in Sydney ignored the lower carrying capacity, and thus the lower revenue-earning capability, of buses, especially compared with Sydney's high-capacity trams. Furthermore, the supposed world-wide trend away from trams was largely confined to English-speaking countries. Many European cities retained and rebuilt their tram networks after the Second World War, with Germany ultimately providing much of the technological base for the later revival of trams in other countries.

In Melbourne in the 1950s – the decade in which the pressure for abolition of trams was greatest – there were some similarities and some differences with Sydney. There were calls for the replacement of trams by politicians returning from overseas, from the media and from others. Melbourne had in fact briefly succumbed to the lure of buses which had replaced some of the last cable lines in the years 1935 to 1940. Also, in the 1950s the 'railway trams' from St Kilda to Brighton Beach and from Sandringham to Black Rock were abandoned in the face of the high cost of renewal, particularly of tracks.

There were, however, key differences between Melbourne and Sydney. Because much of the electric tram system had been inaugurated in the 1920s and 1930s, through the replacement of cable routes, the trams and tracks were generally 20 to 30 years newer than those in Sydney. The trams were of relatively modern design, not reeking of antiquity. And the replacement of cable trams by buses in Bourke Street had been quickly found to be a failure, and had demonstrated the inadequacy of buses in handling very heavy loads.

The key factor in the retention of Melbourne's trams was, however, a notable individual. Sir Robert Risson was Chairman of the Melbourne and Metropolitan Tramways Board from 1949 to 1970. A former Major-General, he was a forceful and effective

DALE BUDD

advocate for trams. In statements, articles and technical papers, an example of which is reproduced later in this book, he documented the advantages of trams. Thus he resisted the pressures from politicians and the media for tram replacement. His leadership was in strong contrast to the situation in Sydney where there were 20 years of indecision, and nobody capable or willing to counter the chattering of those calling for change.

In the 1960s the immediate pressure for the abandonment of trams in Melbourne had passed, but there was reluctance by government to provide funds for new trams to replace the older vehicles in the fleet. Through this decade the trams were well maintained, and tracks were gradually relaid in concrete. This provided a high quality road surface, easing the acceptance of trams by motorists.

By the end of the decade, Melbourne's tram system faced insolvency as a result of declining patronage and rising costs, including the continuing burden, which had also been a factor in Sydney, of maintaining the road between the tracks as well as the tracks themselves. The maintenance and renewals program of the 1960s meant that the physical plant of the system was in good condition. The financial problems could be quickly solved by changes in funding allocations and accounting practices. These paved the way for the eventual renewal of the tram fleet, starting in the mid-1970s.

The importance of leadership was also demonstrated, less happily, in Brisbane. In the 1960s Brisbane had a tram system with characteristics more like those of Melbourne than Sydney. The tracks were in good condition, and the trams were relatively modern. However, the Lord Mayor of the day obtained a 'convenient' report from American consultants, and in a few years the trams were swept away.

The arguments, strong or weak, which led to the abandonment of trams in Sydney and Brisbane, were evident in other Australian cities and led to similar outcomes.

Trams returned to Sydney in 1997 with the opening of a light rail service running initially between Central Station, Darling Harbour and inner suburban Pyrmont. There are also plans afoot for their reinstatement in Brisbane. Under the fashionable new name of light rail, trams are undergoing a widespread revival around the world, not least in Britain and North America. The roundabout has turned full circle. Fortunately, Melbourne had the wisdom never to get off it.

▲ San Diego led the revival of modern tram or light rail development in the USA. Since the first line was opened in 1981 from the city centre to San Ysidro at the Mexican border near Tijuana, the network has steadily expanded. Marketed as the 'San Diego Trolley', the trams are painted in a striking red colour scheme.

Ws, Zs, As and Bs

▼ Fifty years of evolution of tram design is shown by these three trams at the depot in Brunswick. In the centre is W series No 873, built in 1941; at right is Z series No 158, built in 1980; at left is B series No 2057, which first ran in 1990.

RAY MARSH

Melbourne's tram fleet numbers some 500 vehicles, and are of four main types. The oldest are the W series, of which approximately 75 are in service. Additional Ws are held in reserve or in storage, following their replacement by new vehicles. Ws are loosely referred to as the 'W class', but there were originally many different varieties of Ws, classified from W through to W7, and many sub-classes. The first Ws were built in 1923. A wider body style, and improvements such as sliding doors and upholstered seats, came in the 1930s. All of the Ws still in service have these refinements. Apart from the City Circle trams,

the Ws have recently been restored to the green and cream colours dating from the 1920s.

After the last W was built in 1956, a gap of almost 20 years intervened before new trams started arriving on a regular basis. These were the Z series, built between 1975 and 1984. The first Zs were painted in a distinctive orange colour scheme, modified to Deep Yellow in 1979; but 1983 saw the adoption of green and yellow colours. The great majority of the 230 Zs are still in use.

Next came the A series, slightly shorter and with squared off ends, compared with the tapered design of the Zs. There are 70 As, built between 1984 and 1987.

Melbourne's newest trams are the high capacity B series. These have an articulated joint above the centre wheels. The styling of the car body is similar to the A series. Between 1984 and 1994, 132 Bs were built. All but the first two prototypes are air conditioned.

Drawings of the W, Z, A and B series trams appear on pages 32 and 33.

The fleet is operated from eight depots, located at Essendon, Brunswick, Preston, Kew, Camberwell, Malvern, Glenhuntly and Southbank. Overhauls and repairs are undertaken at a large workshop at Preston.

PTCV

KEN CRAVEN

▼ The articulation which is a feature of the B series is illustrated by this picture of No 2111, turning from Spencer Street into Bourke Street. Articulation is commonly used on buses, trams and light rail vehicles overseas, and widely in Australia on buses including a few in Melbourne.

▲ Melbourne's newest tram is B2 class No 2132, seen here on the test track at the plant of the manufacturer, ADtranz, at Dandenong. Like the Z and A series, a B2 has a nominal top speed of 70 km/h.

▲ In the early years of the century, colour schemes for trams, in Melbourne and other cities, often used a combination of dark brown and cream. To recall this bygone era, these colours were applied to A class No 231 in 1993, and the tram for a time carried lettering indicating the 50th anniversary of the Australian Electric Traction Association.

PETER CLARK

▶ About 75 of the popular W series trams remain in service. The oldest have 60 years of operation behind them – well over two million kilometres of service – while the youngest are a mere 40 years old. Cars No 842 and No 845, waiting at South Melbourne Depot for their next turns of duty, display the two colour schemes currently worn by W series trams.

RAY MARSH

Z3 Class
Technical information

Length 16.64 metres
Width 2.67 metres
Height 3.41 metres
Wheelbase 1800 mm truck wheelbase; 8500 mm between
truck centres
Wheel diameter 660 mm
Motors Two 195 kW
Tare 21.8 tonnes
Seats 42 (48 without conductor's consoles)
Builder Commonwealth Engineering Pty Ltd
(Comeng – now ADtranz), Dandenong, Victoria

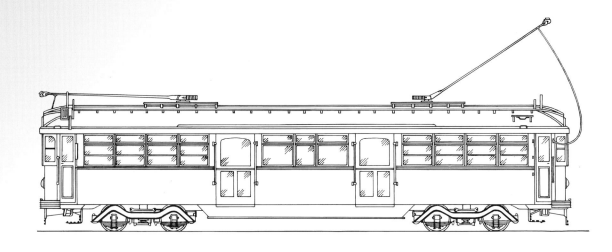

The Z series includes the Z1, Z2 and Z3 classes. The drawing
shows a Z3 class as built. These trams have since been modified by the removal of the conductor's consoles and the
replacement of trolley poles by pantographs, a more modern
means of current collection.

The earlier Z1 and Z2 classes have two doors per side
rather than three. Delays in loading and unloading these earlier Z series trams led to the repositioning of the main exit
door to the centre of the tram on the Z3 class, and the addition of a third door at the rear. The Z3 class also have different electrical equipment from the earlier Zs, and a new design
of suspension giving improved ride quality.

A new numbering system was introduced for the Z series
trams, whose numbers range from 1 to 115 (Z1 and Z2 classes), and from 116 to 230 (Z3 class).

W6 Class
Technical information

Length 14.17 metres
Width 2.73 metres
Height 3.16 metres
Wheelbase 1575 mm truck wheelbase; 8534 mm between
truck centres
Wheel diameter 711 mm
Motors Four 30 kW
Tare 17.7 tonnes
Seats 52
Builder Melbourne and Metropolitan Tramways Board
Workshops, Preston, Victoria

The W6 class are typical of the W series trams currently in
service, which include members of the SW5, SW6, W6 and
W7 classes. The differences between these trams are minor.

The W series trams now in use were built between 1936
and 1956, and their numbers range from 728 to 1039. (The
very last W, No 1040, is in the historic fleet; it is pictured on
page 49). W series trams run on several routes from Swanston
and Collins streets, and on the City Circle service.

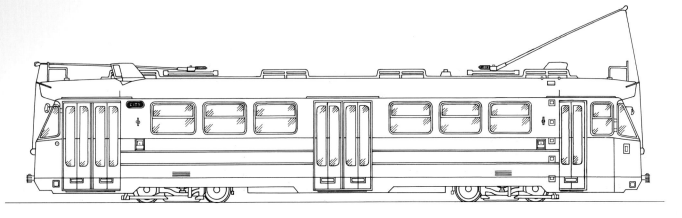

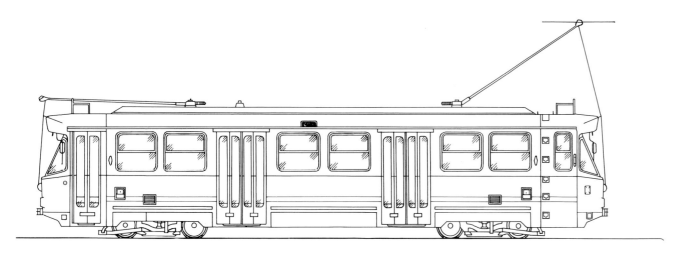

Length   15.01 metres
Width   2.67 metres
Height   3.34 metres
Wheelbase   1800 mm truck wheelbase; 8500 mm between truck centres
Wheel diameter   660 mm
Motors   Two 195 kW
Tare   22.2 tonnes
Seats   42
Builder   Commonwealth Engineering Pty Ltd (Comeng – now ADtranz), Dandenong, Victoria

The body design of the A series features improvements over the Z3 class, with rearranged doors and improved ventilation. The conductor's consoles introduced with the Z series were abandoned in favour of roving conductors. The A2 class differs from the A1 class in having an improved braking system.

The drawing shows an A1 class as built. The later A series trams introduced pantographs to Melbourne's tramways, in place of the traditional trolley poles. Their use is now widespread.

The A series trams operate mainly from Flinders and Collins streets, serving routes including North Balwyn, Mont Albert and Port Melbourne. Their numbers range from 231 to 300.

B2 Class
Technical information

Length   23.63 metres
Width   2.64 metres
Height   3.70 metres
Wheelbase   1800 mm truck wheelbase; 17000 mm between outer truck centres
Wheel diameter   660 mm
Motors   Two 195 kW
Tare   34.0 tonnes
Seats   76
Builder   Commonwealth Engineering Pty Ltd (Comeng) and ASEA Brown Boveri (ABB – now ADtranz), Dandenong, Victoria.

Identified as light rail vehicles, the B2s were ordered for use on the former broad gauge suburban electric railway lines to St Kilda and Port Melbourne, and on newly built extensions to East Burwood and Bundoora which were designed to light rail specifications. The use of B2s has since been extended to other routes.

A B2 class tram has powered trucks (tramway terminology for wheel-sets) under its outer ends, and a non-powered truck under the articulated joint. Two earlier prototype vehicles lack the air-conditioning and dot-matrix destination indicators of the B2 class.

A further new numbering system was introduced with the B series. The two B1 trams are numbered 2001 and 2002, while the B2s are numbered from 2003 to 2132.

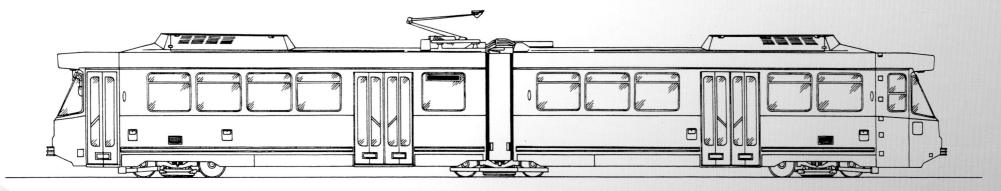

TRAMS in ART and ART on TRAMS

ARTS VICTORIA

In 1978 the Ministry of Transport and the Ministry for the Arts launched a program entitled Transporting Art, involving the painting of trams by noted artists. The program was the brainchild of noted artist Clifton Pugh and the then Lord Mayor of Melbourne, Irvin Rockman. The Ministry for the Arts selected 16 artists and paid their fees. The Tramways Board provided paint, workshop space and 16 W series trams.

In 1986 a second series of 15 Transporting Art trams was launched. Most of this group was sponsored by major companies or by the Victorian Health Promotion Foundation.

None of the Transporting Art trams are currently in service, although several are in storage and the very first painted tram, by Clifton Pugh, is destined for the Museum of Victoria.

A separate 'thematic' program provided an opportunity for state government departments, statutory authorities and local government to suggest themes for promotion using painted trams, in this case the Z series as well as the older W cars.

Apart from these uses of trams as a base for artistic expression, a number of distinguished artists have included trams in paintings, either as a central theme or as incidental elements in a wider setting. This is a further recognition of the importance of trams to Melbourne and to the lives of Melburnians.

▲ Tram No 731, painted by Lesley Dumbrell, poses for its official photograph on Queens Bridge.

▶ David Larwill working on the roof of his tram. Artists painted their trams in the paint shop at Preston Workshops.

ARTS VICTORIA

▲ Tram No 567, one of the original Transporting Art series, immediately after it was painted at Preston Workshops. The Rising Sun emblem and the wording 'Sayonara Koala' on Peter Corrigan's tram created a controversy and complaints from the Japanese community, leading to the painting-out of the Japanese flags and their replacement by white or grey rectangles.

▲ Tram No 738, by Jeffrey Makin, on Spencer Street bridge.

▼ Decorated in 1990, the 'Koorie' tram promoted Victoria's Aboriginal cultural heritage.

◄ 'The apostle birds in flight, as if the tram has run into a group of them and they're flying along the sides. Then I found the route was to be through Hawthorn and Collingwood football territory, and one cannot be one-eyed in that world, so there is a magpie and a hawk on each side!' Clifton Pugh so described the first tram in the Transporting Art program, which he painted in 1978.

▲ Anne Graham:
Autumn in Melbourne
1987–88
Oil on canvas
365 cm x 122 cm.

◀ Tram No 721 by Steig
Persson, posing for the
photographer on the
Esplanade at St Kilda.

Red is the predominant colour for this Transporting Art tram painted by Craig Gough, who described his design as follows: 'I visualised the tram as an exciting and joyous object only seen briefly as it trundled past. I chose red as the dominant colour idea and then augmented this with a chord structure of supporting hues, reflecting my concern with colour and lyricism, not unlike jazz music. I attempted the strongest intensity and vibration of redness that I could muster and to tune melody, harmony and rhythm in such a way that in the grey of Melbourne's winter it could be like a riotous jazz band.'

Thematic tram No 727, painted in 1989 for the Spoleto Festival.

Not Bourke Street, Melbourne, but Bourke Street, Mount Buller, one of the mountain's most popular ski lifts.

▲ Michael Leunig applying the finishing touches to his tram.

▶ First of the second series of Transporting Art trams, painted by Michael Leunig, poses at Luna Park.

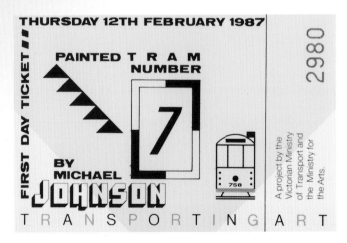

FIRST DAY TICKET

THURSDAY 12TH FEBRUARY 1987

PAINTED T R A M NUMBER

7

BY MICHAEL JOHNSON

2980

758

A project by the Victorian Ministry of Transport and the Ministry for the Arts.

T R A N S P O R T I N G A R T

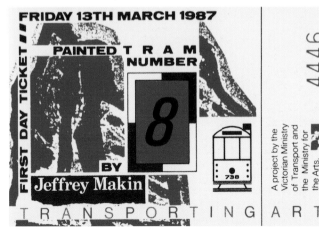

FIRST DAY TICKET

FRIDAY 13TH MARCH 1987

PAINTED T R A M NUMBER

8

BY Jeffrey Makin

4446

738

A project by the Victorian Ministry of Transport and the Ministry for the Arts.

T R A N S P O R T I N G A R T

FIRST DAY TICKET

MONDAY 3RD NOVEMBER 1986

PAINTED T R A M NUMBER

5

BY LESLEY dumbrell

2515

731

A project by the Victorian Ministry of Transport and the Ministry for the Arts.

T R A N S P O R T I N G A R T

▽ Robert Jacks poses with his tram.

ARTS VICTORIA

◀ No 829 near Luna Park, route 69 terminus, painted in 1986 for the International Year of Peace.

▽ No 441, painted to mark Victoria's 150th anniversary in 1984, passing the Queen Victoria Hospital in Swanston Street. This colourful tram now runs in Bendigo.

DAVID KEENAN

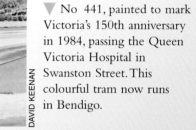

▽ Tram No 760 by Robert Jacks, against the picturesque backdrop of the City Courts in La Trobe Street.

ARTS VICTORIA

RAY MARSH

▲ Stewart Merrett:
Peak Hour 1986
Aplekage mural.

▶ Lesley Dumbrell's
brightly painted tram at its
launch ceremony in the
Bourke Street Mall.

◀ Centre section of Merrin
Eirth's eye-catching tram.

▲ John Brack,
born Australia 1920:
The Tram 1952
Oil on canvas
60 cm x 81 cm.

▼ Two painted trams pass
at the northern end of
Swanston Street. No 738
was painted by Jeffrey Makin,
while No 806 is the work of
Elizabeth Gower.

▲ Eric Fennemore:
A Melbourne Scene.

IN THE SUBURBS

A ride on the West Coburg tram takes passengers through Royal Park, a large expanse of land set aside in the early days of settlement. Royal Park includes the Zoological Gardens, an 18 hole golf course and a multitude of sporting ovals and facilities.

SWIMMING CLASS TICKET

Good only for a single journey on any Route

Not good on Public Holidays nor during School Vacations.

Swimming Class Ticket Conductor must detach and retain this portion of Ticket.

MELB. & METRO. TRAMWAYS BOARD

▶ Public transport in abundance: Trams on the West Coburg line pass under the rail overbridge at Royal Park while a veteran suburban electric train speeds towards Flemington Bridge en route to the city.

DAVID MACARTNEY

DOUG COLQUHOUN

▲ With its livery blending almost perfectly with the adjacent flora, a tram emerges from under the railway viaduct en route to the city.

▼ Slipping between the fairways and bunkers of the Royal Park Golf Course, a tram heads north towards Brunswick and West Coburg.

▼ A tram driver pauses to check for road traffic at Park Street, the northern boundary of Royal Park, before climbing the short grade to Brunswick Road.

▼ Two L class trams ordered by the Prahran and Malvern Tramways Trust shortly after the end of the First World War were still in use in the mid-1990s, operating on Sundays between the city and the Zoo. Here, No 106, painted in its original colour scheme, prepares to return to the city, having discharged its passengers at the Zoo's rear entrance.

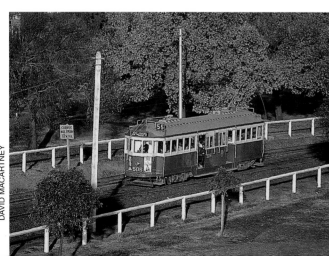

DAVID MACARTNEY

W J McNIVEN

DAVID KEENAN

DAVID MACARTNEY

RAY MARSH

▶ Victoria Parade, East Melbourne, ranks with St Kilda Road and Royal Parade as one of the city's most attractive avenues. Amid autumn colours, a tram accelerates up Victoria Parade towards the city.

W J McNIVEN

▲ Reflected momentarily in trackside water, No 246 catches the full western sun as it speeds along the tramway reservation towards Essendon Aerodrome. Poles for overhead wiring on this part of the Essendon line were shortened and painted conspicuously because of the line's close proximity to the east-west runway.

▶ No 585 waits for passengers at the intersection of Hawthorn Road and the Nepean Highway, East Brighton. Until the reintroduction of tram services in Christchurch, New Zealand, in 1995, this location was for many years the most southerly point of tramway operation in the world.

RANDALL WILSON

▲ The way forward: Articulated B series trams operate a fast and frequent service on Melbourne's latest tramway extension to the outer northern destination of Bundoora–RMIT.

▶ With a squeal from its wheels, a tram turns into Fletcher Street, Essendon, before heading west to busy Mount Alexander Road.

DAVID MACARTNEY

W L WILLIAMS

BRIAN ANDREWS

▲ The way we were: In the late 1960s, No 374, a member of the 406-strong W2 class, heads south along Glenferrie Road with over 40 years service behind it. Route 69, which connects St Kilda Beach with Cotham Road, Kew, is one of only four cross-suburban routes in Melbourne.

SCHOLARS TICKETS

◄ The undulations of Melbourne's eastern suburbs establish this vista along Riversdale Road, Camberwell, from the railway crossing (in the foreground, with its distinctive boom barriers), to St Dominic's Church on the horizon.

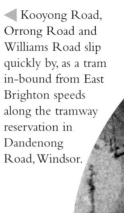 Kooyong Road, Orrong Road and Williams Road slip quickly by, as a tram in-bound from East Brighton speeds along the tramway reservation in Dandenong Road, Windsor.

▲ With through lines and double curves on every corner, the junction at Balaclava is a 'grand union', a unique and impressive feature of Melbourne's tramway system. Built in 1913 by the Prahran and Malvern Tramways Trust, the junction was the means by which several of the Trust's routes reached Caulfield, Elsternwick and St Kilda Beach, then key points on its network.

◀ The junction in use: No 954 turns from Hawthorn Road towards Darling Road, East Malvern, while another tram prepares to turn north towards its destination of Cotham Road, Kew.

Drivers, conductors and local boys idle their way through a hot summer afternoon as they wait for cricket fans to fill trams in Albert Road, South Melbourne.

DAVID MACARTNEY

With 'Racecourse' and 'Special' shown as their destinations, trams manoeuvre to pick up city-bound punters from Caulfield Racecourse.

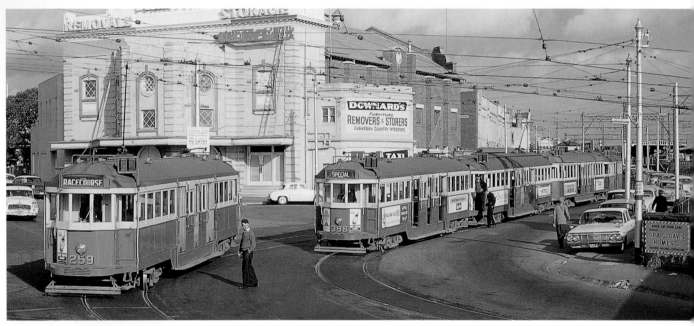

W J McNIVEN

In the days when the Swans were synonymous with South Melbourne rather than Sydney, the team was based at South Melbourne and trams showing 'Football' as their destination were part of the action. Loyal fans make their way to trams waiting in nearby Albert Road on a Saturday when 'South played at South'.

48

Tram drivers are made, not born. Staff turnover means that tramway authorities are constantly engaged in driver training to maintain services. Showing 'Special' on the destination sign and an instructor by his side, a student tries his hand on No 1040, the last of 756 W series trams built for Melbourne.

DALE BUDD

C D ROBERTSON

Having completed its westward journey along Victoria Street, a tram swings north into Errol Street, North Melbourne, en route to its destination of West Maribyrnong.

JEREMY WAINWRIGHT

Having discharged its load of fun-seekers, a tram waits in the siding opposite Luna Park on a summer night in the early 1960s. In a few minutes, the crew will be on board and No 363 will have disappeared into the night, bound for the northern destination of Kew – Cotham Road.

St Kilda Junction has been a key intersection in Melbourne for well over a century. In this scene dating from 1912, a cable tram pauses before heading north along St Kilda Road to the city.

(and opposite page, left) In the years following the Second World War, peak period traffic congestion at St Kilda Junction grew steadily worse until priority was given in the mid-1960s to the total reconstruction of the intersection. Undertaken over several years, the work involved extensive land resumption and building demolition, numerous detours and completion of the grade separation works which form the basis of the present arterial roads.

The photographs on the opposite page (bottom) and this page (left and bottom left) trace the recent history of St Kilda Junction, from the mid–1950s and early 1960s, through the early period of its redevelopment, to its present form.

Built by the Melbourne and Hobson's Bay United Railway Company, the broad gauge railways to Port Melbourne (formerly Sandridge) and St Kilda were the oldest in the State. In 1987, however, poor patronage and deteriorating infrastructure resulted in the integration of these lines into the tram network. With railway overhead wiring structures apparent in the distance and oversized sleepers visible in the foreground, two A series trams pass near Albert Park shortly after trams took over services on the St Kilda line.

THE HISTORIC FLEET

Trams have been designed, built and modified over many years to meet a variety of requirements. Representatives of many of older types now form the basis of a historic fleet which recalls how previous generations of Melburnians travelled.

WILLIAM F SCOTT

▼ Built in 1916 for the Hawthorn Tramways Trust, No 8 spent only 14 years in Melbourne before being sold to the State Electricity Commission for use in Bendigo. Returned to Melbourne, it was restored to near-original condition at Preston Workshops.

▲ Although a very basic form of rail transport, horse-drawn trams offered passengers a superior ride to horse-drawn buses which had to negotiate the rough and pot-holed surfaces of many nineteenth century roads. A vehicle similar to this enabled Melburnians to reach the Zoo in Royal Park from the intersection of Gatehouse Street and Royal Parade between 1890 until 1923 when the service came to an abrupt end following a depot fire during a police strike.

▼ Some of Hawthorn Depot's occupants on display in 1992. Closed to routine operations in 1965, the depot has been used for interim storage of some members of the historic fleet.

HAWTHORN TRAMWAYS TRUST

8

RANDALL WILSON

SHANE MOORE

Melbourne's last single-truck trams were built in 1930 to improve service standards on short-distance lines such as Point Ormond and the Footscray system. No 676 presents an image of modernity as it passes a slow-moving 'Ransome' steam wagon in Wellington Parade.

▲ Lined up at South Melbourne Depot, all six members of the L class pose for a family portrait in 1975. Nos 104 and 106 have been retained in the historic fleet.

▶ Passengers on W1 class trams in the 1920s were able to enjoy open-air seating reminiscent of cable grip-cars, then being replaced by electric trams. Popular in warm weather but less satisfactory in winter, the open centre section was enclosed a little more than a decade after W1s' introduction in 1925.

GLEN MILLS

RAY MARSH

DAVID WILSON

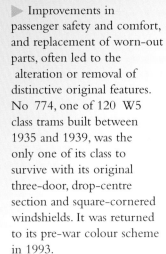

Improvements in passenger safety and comfort, and replacement of worn-out parts, often led to the alteration or removal of distinctive original features. No 774, one of 120 W5 class trams built between 1935 and 1939, was the only one of its class to survive with its original three-door, drop-centre section and square-cornered windshields. It was returned to its pre-war colour scheme in 1993.

RANDALL WILSON

▲ Nos 469 and 613 were among a small group of experimental trams built in 1927 and 1930 that reflected design trends in North America.

▼ In these trams, passengers could see the driver in action.

▼ Two veterans pass in La Trobe Street during a tramway cavalcade in 1979. The envy of many a museum, Birney tram No 217 represents a distinctive American design of the 1920s. Heading for East Melbourne is No 14, formerly operated by the Prahran and Malvern Tramways Trust, and visiting from Ballarat.

W J McNIVEN

W J McNIVEN

No 214 was one of the largest and fastest vehicles on the road in 1906 when it entered service with the North Melbourne Electric Tramways and Lighting Company. In 1978, after more than 50 years as a freight tram (see page 15), No 214 was reconverted to a 'toast-rack' passenger tram and restored to near-original condition. The oldest electric tram in Melbourne, it is seen here in Wellington Parade, East Melbourne, with another representative vehicle of its era.

Built in 1917 for the Melbourne, Brunswick and Coburg Tramways Trust, T class No 180 crosses the intersection of Market Street and Flinders Street.

From 1928 until withdrawals began in earnest in the 1970s, the W2 class were synonymous with Melbourne transport. Resplendent in Hawthorn Green and Cream, No 510 presents the classic appearance of tram travel in the early post-war years.

Magnificently restored to the original 1923 W class design, distinguished by three equal-width doorways, No 380 poses for its portrait in Simpson Street, East Melbourne.

CARE and MAINTENANCE

Like other major undertakings, Melbourne's tramways require facilities and staff committed to carrying out maintenance and improvements, and where appropriate, preserving trams and other items of historic significance.

▶ Despite the advent of innovations such as dot-matrix indicators, many trams retain fabric destination rolls. What appears to be white lettering on a black background is actually produced by applying black paint to a white surface to produce the required combination of suburb and street names. Midway through the task, a painter at Preston Workshops prepares new rolls for use in W-series. trams.

RANDALL WILSON

▶ In the 1990s, Z, A and B series trams have become the backbone of the Melbourne fleet, supplemented by W series trams. Gone are some interesting variants from the past such as the L class, represented by No 106, and No 52, acquired in 1959 from the Victorian Railways following closure of the St Kilda–Brighton Beach line. Still running today is works tram No 10, at left, beside Z series No 10, its junior by some 67 years.

R S JONES

TRAM ALIVE

DANGER

RAY MARSH

ROBERT BELZER

▲ A wet evening at Kew Depot.

▶ A tram edges its way along temporary track in Balaclava Road in the late 1960s.

▲ Spared the hazards of weekday congestion, track workers relay a section of track in Collins Street on a quiet Sunday morning.

TRAMS RUNNING OUT OF DEPOT MUST GIVE WAY TO TRAMS RUNNING INTO DEPOT

BRIAN ANDREWS

DRIVERS UNTIE ROPES & RELEASE FROM CLIPS

Built in 1908, the same year as the first T-model Ford, track maintenance trams Nos 10W and 11W began their existence as 'toast-rack' passenger trams in Sydney, similar to No 1296 seen here at Mosman Wharf in 1953.

NOEL REED

RAY MARSH

Kew Depot: Veteran W series trams, symbols of Melbourne.

HUGH WALDRON

First tram on a new line: Engineers and technicians check the progress of No 11W as it edges its way towards Bundoora–RMIT, in August 1995.

Since 1975 Melbourne's trams have been built by ADtranz or its predecessor companies at Dandenong. New trams were transported in near-complete form across Melbourne by semi-trailer to Preston Workshops where they were made ready for traffic. With lining, logos and numbers yet to be applied, workers prepare to move a new articulated tram onto the transfer ramp.

Until the advent of purpose-built road vehicles, track maintenance was traditionally performed using trams designed or modified for the task. Regarded as mobile monstrosities by passers-by, these vehicles undertook important functions such as the removal of sand and dirt from rail grooves, rail welding and grinding, and general track cleaning. Only a few remain in use, mainly to clean the rail surface.

Track cleaning tram No 7W in High Street, St Kilda, in February 1959.

Ready to roll: 2110 and 2106 undergo final inspection as they await their first tour of duty in January 1993.

THEN and NOW

The Met

▲ End of the working week: With the clocks on Flinders Street Station showing 12.20 pm on a Saturday, pedestrians, trams and horse-drawn wagons compete for road space. When this picture was taken in 1927, electric trams had taken over in Swanston Street but the cable trams on the Richmond line still ran in Flinders Street.

RANDALL WILSON

ROBERT BELZER

RANDALL WILSON

▲ The scene from the same vantage point 68 years later. Three of the four structures, Flinders Street Station, Young and Jackson's Hotel and St Paul's Cathedral remain as familiar landmarks for future generations. The advent of the underground rail loop has made this less of a focal point for commuters.

▶ By the 1990s the unattractive twin towers and elevated windswept plaza built 30 years earlier as part of the Princes Gate project had become objects of derision. They were demolished by early 1997.

These photos record for posterity the view from the rooftops of the buildings, first in 1969, and then in 1995 with the Arts Centre built on part of the former City Road alignment

The formation of the Bourke Street Mall between Swanston and Elizabeth Streets in the mid-1970s signified a return to placing the interests of pedestrians ahead of the motor vehicle for the first time in many years.

◀▼ By 1984 this section of Bourke Street had been enhanced very considerably by colourful paving and planter tubs and seating. The result contrasts with the congested conditions faced by No 999 in 1968.

▶▼ In the early 1970s, some years before their conversion to light rail, the St Kilda and Port Melbourne railway lines were the domain of the Victorian Railways' most antiquated carriages. (right) A swing-door electric train crosses Albert Road, South Melbourne shortly before the withdrawal of this type of rollingstock in 1974. (below) A light rail vehicle passes the same location in 1996.

▶ (far right) Apart from peak periods, patronage on the St Kilda line rarely required trains of more than two carriages. One such train, and its successor, a B series tram, are seen here leaving South Melbourne.

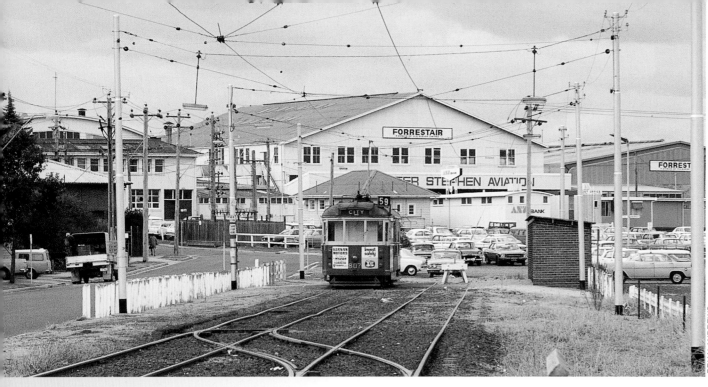

BRIAN ANDREWS

◀ A distinguishing feature of Melbourne's tram system is that relatively little track has been closed. One of the few instances is the last few hundred metres of the former line to Essendon Aerodrome. It was closed in 1976 when the route was diverted to Airport West, and today almost no evidence remains of the track leading to the former terminus.

DALE BUDD

W J McNIVEN

▲ The Wattle Park line beyond Warrigal Road was among the last routes to be provided with double track, and the service was further

The eastward extension of the Burwood line to Middleborough Road in 1978 was the first significant addition to Melbourne's tram system in 22 years. Built to light-rail rather than traditional tramway specifications, the new line enabled tram users to enjoy the improved engineering standards then being applied to the Burwood Highway and other outer suburban roads. The newness of the line and the reconstructed highway is evident in the first scene, showing a Z series tram near Elgar Road shortly after the extension opened. With the landscape softened by 17 years growth of trees and other vegetation, the second view shows an articulated B series tram at the same location in 1995.

IAN HAMMOND

JEREMY WAINWRIGHT

DALE BUDD

improved a few years later with the advent of new trams. Old and new are contrasted in these views from the late 1960s and the mid 1980s.

ROAD VEHICLES

FOUR MILES PER HOUR.

NO ROAD

P W DUCKETT

Trams first crossed the Maribyrnong River in 1940 to serve the explosives factory at West Maribyrnong. For the next 27 years, an unusual feature of the river crossing was the existance of separate road and tramway bridges, which confused more than the occasional unsuspecting motorist on a drizzly Saturday night!

◀▼ Built originally as a single track bridge, the tramway viaduct was dupli- cated in 1943, in line with the growth in wartime traffic on the West Maribyrnong

JEREMY WAINWRIGHT

ARTHUR PERRY

CARS STOP HERE

57

CITY VIA MOON MELB

EMPLOYMENT SEFURITY TRAMWAY SERVICE

KEEP LEFT

DO NOT FOLLOW TRAMS

▶▼ As road traffic increased, so did the number of detour signs, until a new bridge for both motor vehicles and trams was completed in 1967.

JEREMY WAINWRIGHT

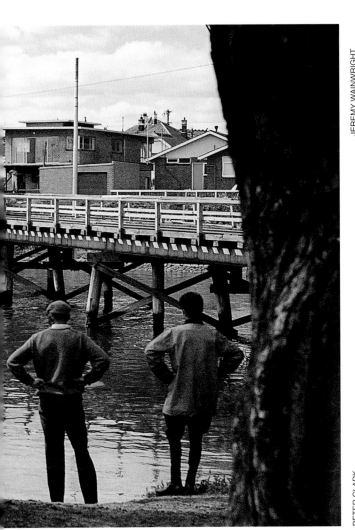

PETER CLARK

A PREMIER CITY for TRAMS

Melbourne's tram system is large by international standards, although its ranking against overseas systems varies, depending on the basis of comparison. Using the criteria of fleet size, route kilometres and number of serviced lines, the only cities with systems larger than Melbourne's on the bases of all three criteria are St Petersburg, Bucharest, Moscow and Kiev, in that order. Melbourne therefore has the largest tram system of any English-speaking country, and the largest outside Europe and the former USSR. It could also be said to have, in approximate terms, the fifth largest tram system in the world.

In reaching these conclusions the difficulties of making international comparisons should be borne in mind. Tramway authorities measure the extent of their operations differently, and the reported size of tram fleets may be inflated significantly by the existence of a high proportion of small or unserviceable vehicles. The figure for Melbourne's fleet in the accompanying table includes about 70 trams which are either held in reserve or are stored. This number is low compared with some eastern European systems listed in the table.

▶ The avenue of Canary Island date palms in Mount Alexander Road, Essendon, contrasts with the deciduous trees planted in tramway reservations nearer the city. No 683 heads for Essendon Aerodrome, the only airport in Australia served by trams.

▶ San Francisco was the first city to introduce cable trams, in 1873. Today, the city has the last three cable lines operating anywhere in the world. No other form of traction can match the performance of the cable trams on the precipitous grades which are a feature of San Francisco's topography. The diminutive vehicles are a feature of the city, used by commuters and tourists alike.

HOW THE SIZE OF MELBOURNE'S TRAM FLEET COMPARES INTERNATIONALLY

Ranking	City	Country	Size of tram fleet	Route (kilometres)	Number of lines
1	St Petersburg	Russia	2146	678	66
2	Vienna	Austria	1040	195	35
3	Kiev	Ukraine	1000	273	26
4	Prague	Czech Republic	918	453	21
5	Moscow	Russia	851	386	32
6	Bucharest	Romania	834	398	43
7	Berlin	Germany	788	178	25
8	Milan	Italy	642	199	18
9	Melbourne	Australia	567	241	25
10	Tashkent	Uzbekistan	490	228	28
11	Odessa	Ukraine	450	259	24
12	Wroclaw	Poland	447	270	33
13	Niznij Novgorod	Russia	442	183	19
14	Sofia	Bulgaria	420	158	16
15	Poznan	Poland	396	243	13
16	Brussels	Belgium	330	199	15
17	Novosibirsk	Siberia	300	354	18
18	Ostrava	Czech Republic	287	231	18
19	Bratislava	Slovakia	247	255	12
20	Alma-Ata	Kazakhstan	110	210	9

Source: *Jane's Urban Transport 1996–97* and Public Transport Corporation of Victoria.

DALE BUDD

▲ For many years Brussels was a leader in tramway development in Europe. Its trams used the latest technology adapted from the USA, and were modern, fast and comfortable. A number of lines were placed underground in the city centre, a trend which later fell from favour as the benefits of accessibility at street level were better appreciated.

▼ East German cities continued to build and use small trams long after large vehicles had become universal elsewhere. Berlin has a very large fleet of trams, and still retains a handful of smaller vehicles.

A dinky four-wheeler is seen arriving at the picturesque Woltersdorf terminus in Berlin, in a charming 1996 scene which has changed little over the previous 40 years.

◀ Much rebuilt over the years, these colourful four-wheelers, seen in Des Voeux Road in Hong Kong's central district, seem certain to continue in service well into the 21st century.

RANDALL WILSON

HOWARD CLARK

WHAT MIGHT HAVE BEEN

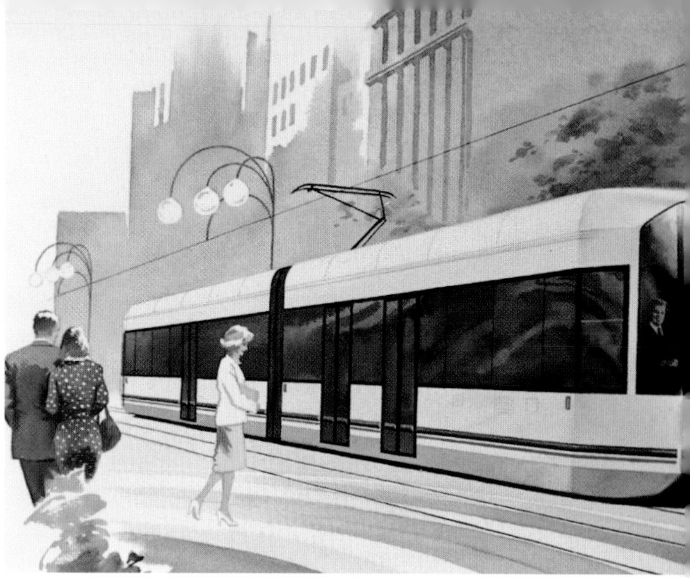

After the consolidation of most of the tramway network under the control of the Melbourne and Metropolitan Tramways Board, a fleet of 756 W series trams was built between 1923 and 1956. Tram design followed a logical progression, with the introduction of upholstered seats, sliding doors and other improvements in the 1930s. Very few non-standard trams were acquired, including 18 four-wheel trams for lightly-loaded routes or all-night services, and five larger trams introduced in 1927 and 1930 for experiments with driver-only operations.

Behind this evolution in design were a large number of concepts which were prepared, refined, evaluated and then (except in the case of those brought into production) discarded.

Here are some glimpses of trams which never were.

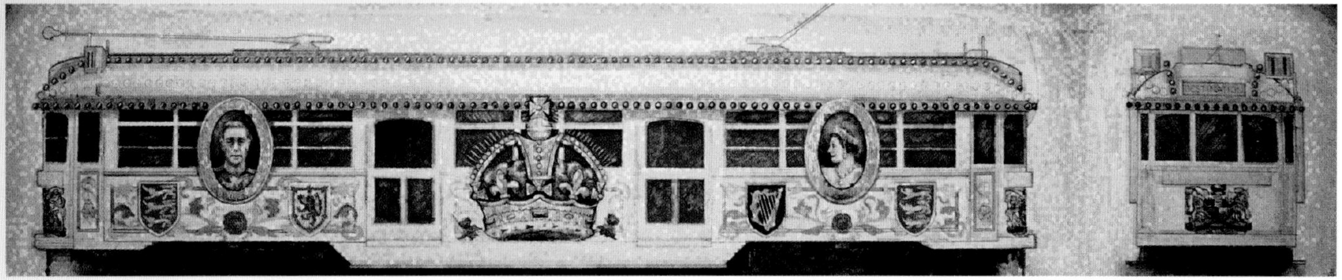

DALE BUDD

◀ The death of King George VI in 1952 caused the cancellation of a planned royal tour of Australia, and as a result this design for an attractively decorated tram never saw the light of day.

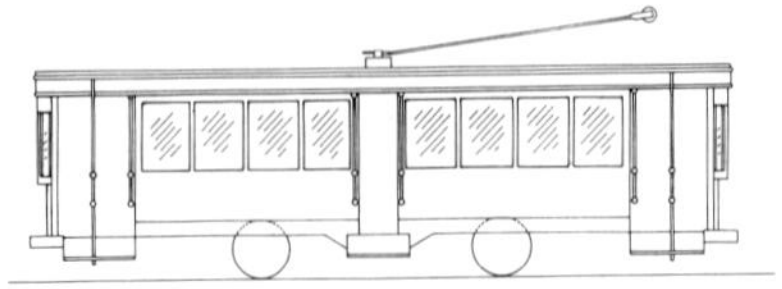

▲ The design of this diminutive four-wheeler was considered in the 1920s. Ultimately a much more stylish form was adopted.

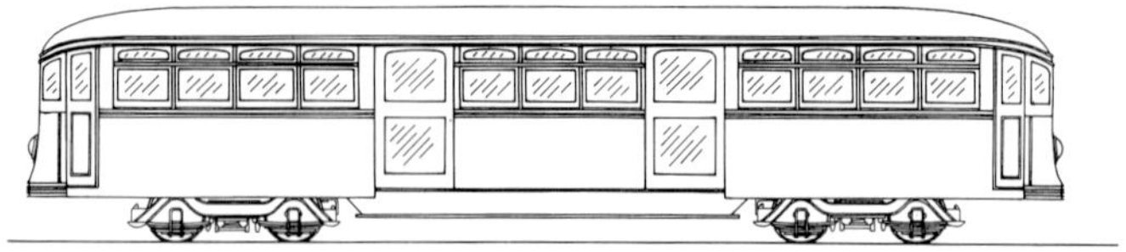

▲ Many of the styling concepts revealed in the drawings held in the files at Preston Workshops reveal the influence of North American trends in tram design. Curved ends and arches above the windows are among American design features of the 1920s and 1930s. Few of these concepts found their way into the final design of trams for Melbourne, which retained a distinctive Australian appearance.

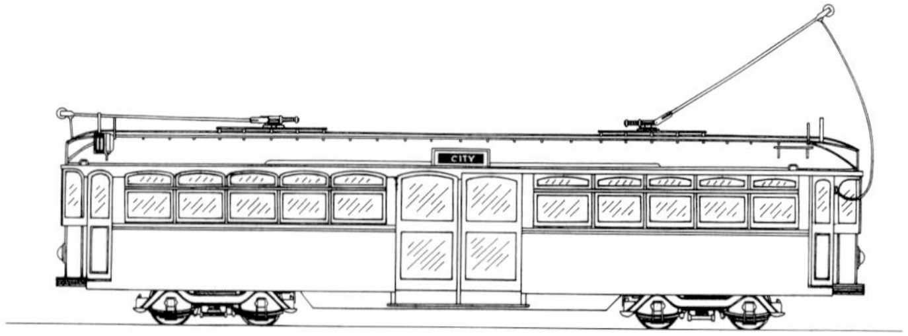

▲ An alternative to the later W series introduced in the 1930s was this design, with a single large doorway in the centre and North American styling features.

In 1990 it was proposed that the later units of the B series should incorporate a low floor in the centre section to reduce the number and height of the steps encountered by passengers. This artist's impression shows the appearance of the modified form. In the event, cost considerations led to abandonment of the low floor concept, and the entire B series was built to the original high-floor design.

PHIL BELBIN, COURTESY JOHN DUNN/ADTRANZ

JEREMY WAINWRIGHT

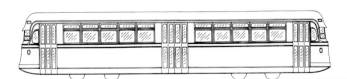

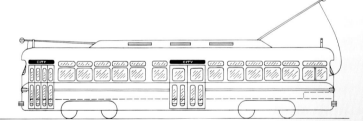

These two tram proposals recall bus designs of the 1930s and 1940s – but in fact it was trams, in North America, which introduced this styling prior to its later use on buses. The drawing on the right reflects the appearance of a modern North American tram of the 1930s.

In 1962 the Melbourne and Metropolitan Tramways Board proposed a scheme for trams in the central city area to be placed underground. Tunnels were to run beneath Swanston and Bourke streets, prohibitive costs led to the plan being abandoned. Since then the benefits of trams running at street level have been widely appreciated and the notion of putting trams underground, where they are less accessible, has fallen from favour.

MOBILE BILLBOARDS

Eye-catching advertisements have adorned Melbourne's trams since the 1950s. For many years, a single tram was available for complete repainting as a moving advertisement. Today, a dozen trams at a time are transformed by an advertising concept. Known as 'supertrams' in the advertising industry, these colourful trams add variety to city streets.

▲ A zany promotion for the Royal Show.

▲ The use of trams for advertising began early with a tram used to promote recruitment during the First World War, as shown on page 16. In the 1940s trams were occasionally used for special campaigns, which tended to be community-based rather than commercially oriented, such as this savings campaign in 1945.

▶ The 'Parade of Homes' exhibition in the mid-1950s was promoted by this large sign on a tram which doubled as a freight tram, carrying stores from Preston Workshops to the various tram depots throughout Melbourne.

PTCV

PTCV

PTCV

Well-chosen words promote *Les Miserables* on a tram photographed against the mellow brickwork of Malvern Depot.

Techniques developed in recent years enable an advertisement to extend across a tram's windows. A giant tiger entices visitors to the zoo, and a campaign for the Royal Australian Navy.

OLYMPICS FOR MELBOURNE 1996

RAY MARSH

BUSPAK

▲ This articulated tram was brightly painted for a proposed housing development at Port Melbourne.

▼▶ For many years one W series tram was fitted with rows of lights along its roof for special use in advertising. In these two campaigns the tram was painted in the corporate colours associated with the product being promoted: a red theme for Johnny Walker Red Label; and gold for the Benson & Hedges Centenary Cricket Test in 1977, some years before the banning of tobacco advertising.

▲ If colourful design on a tram had been the yardstick, Melbourne should have won its bid for the 1996 Olympic Games.

CITY

Johnnie Walker Red Label

Born 1820

Still going strong

PTCV

◀ Chinese red provides a great visual impact on the tram painted in 1988 to promote both Melbourne's relationship with its sister city, Jiangsu, and the associated visit of pandas to the Melbourne Zoo.

INDULGENCES

RESTAURANTS, FILMS AND WEDDINGS...

GLEN MILLS

▼ The Colonial Tramcar Company's Restaurant trams have become a distinctive feature of the city. Since the venture began in 1982, the restaurant fleet has grown to three vehicles, each with seating for 36 patrons. Excellent food is complemented by the stylish fitout of these trams, which are popular with individuals and groups alike.

▼ The film *Malcolm* centred on the exploits of a tram buff whose ability with gadgets led to a successful criminal career. In this scene, filmed at the depot at South Melbourne, Colin Friels in the title role is setting off with his homemade tram for an early morning run.

▲ Among the more unusual uses of trams are those for weddings. These two tram enthusiasts hired a four-wheeler for the occasion, complete with white ribbon and a destination sign displaying the location of a tram museum in Britain.

▶ Colin Friels, John Hargreaves and Lindy Davies pose with the later version of Malcolm's unusual getaway tram. *Malcolm* was directed by Nadia Tass and released by Cascade Films in 1986.

COLONIAL TRAMCAR COMPANY

CASCADE FILMS

Melbourne's streets are filled with restaurants.

At a slumbering 20 kph on a super absorbent suspension system, it's hardly fast food. But even at this pace, a 5 star meal on the only mobile tramcar restaurant in the world will go by too quickly.

And with good reason. As soon as you enter this 1927 vintage world class tram, with its luxurious Pullman style decor and mouth watering dishes of all Victorian produce, you'll wish it never stopped. You can catch it for a 3 to 5 course lunch or dinner. Even the view has several courses to choose from - Toorak Road, Fitzroy Street, Acland Street,

Victoria Street and Southgate - are just a few of the directions you can go. And these destinations are not just for the Restaurant tram.

They're just some of the fabulous culinary routes you can travel down for a memorable dining experience in Melbourne. There's everything from

Japanese to Zulu, from Malaysian to Hungarian.

If you love great food and haven't experienced Melbourne's restaurant circuit ask for a menu.

Call Tourism Victoria on 1 800 63 77 63 for your free copy of The Melbourne Brochure.

You'll love every piece of Victoria

MOJO TOV 102

GONE BUT NOT FORGOTTEN

Except for the 1960s the size of the electric tram network in Melbourne has grown every decade this century. It is fortunate that the few closures which occurred in the post-war years did not mark the beginning of a general contraction of the system.

Operated as a separate entity from 1921, the Footscray lines were isolated from the main tramway system until connecting track was laid in Maidstone in 1954. The combination of small, four-wheel trams and three short lines gave the system a quaintness that resembled the tramways of Ballarat, Bendigo and Geelong.

In Melbourne's bayside suburbs, the Victorian Railways operated two 'electric street railways'. The first of these, which opened in 1906, was a broad-gauge line (1600mm gauge) between St Kilda railway station and Brighton Beach railway station. This line was the first successful electric tramway in Melbourne, following the short-lived Box Hill–Doncaster line which operated from 1889 to 1896. The second Victorian Railways line, which opened in 1919, was of standard gauge and ran between Sandringham and Black Rock. From 1926 to 1931, this line extended a further 3.5 km to Beaumaris.

As a minor adjunct to the state's rail services, the 'railway trams' never enjoyed the attention given to their counterparts elsewhere in Melbourne. Low investment and sporadic interest by railway administrators led to the closure of the Sandringham-Black Rock line in 1956, followed by the closure of the St Kilda-Brighton Beach line in 1959.

A shuttle service operated along Glenhuntly Road between Point Ormond and Elsternwick railway station until October 1960 when it was replaced by a bus service.

Built by the Victorian Railways Newport Workshops in 1917, brand new bogie tram No 28 shows off its striking livery outside Elwood Depot.

PTCV

With passengers from the connecting bus service on board, No 48 will shortly depart Black Rock for Sandringham, 4 km to the north.

HUGH BALLMENT

For over 50 years St Kilda station served as an interchange point between suburban trains and the feeder tramway.

As summer twilight turns to evening, a tram waits for passengers at St Kilda station during the final weeks of the Brighton Beach line.

PTCV

JIM SELETTO

Different appearance, different gauges, different management. Victorian Railways bogie tram No 43 meets No 894 of the Melbourne and Metropolitan Tramways Board as it clunks across the standard gauge track in Fitzroy Street to reach St Kilda railway station.

E SKILLER

POINT ORMOND
ELSTERNWICK R^{LY} S^{TN}
SOUTH CAULFIELD J^{UN}
GLENH^{TLY} DEPOT
SPECIAL

DAVID KEENAN

◀ Unfazed by local traffic, a tram driver goes about his task of picking up and setting down passengers in Barkly Street, en route to Russell Street, West Footscray.

◀ On a clear autumn day in 1957, a tram waits for passengers at Point Ormond terminus, set in parkland near Point Ormond Road.

JIM SELETO

ARTHUR PERRY

Footscray trams could be readily distinguished from others in Melboune by their destination signs, which included 'Pyrotechnic Factory', 'Explosives Factory' and other intriguing locations.

EXPLOSIVES FTY
ORDNANCE FTY
DEPOT
WILLIAMSTOWN RD
RAILWAY STATION
RUSSELL ST
BALLARAT RD
SPECIAL
FOOTBALL GROUND
AMMUNITION FTY
PYROTECHNIC FTY
CITY VIA HAYMARKET
SPECIAL. E

▲ Bound for Ballarat Road, No 465 swings from Hopkins Street into Droop Street in the early 1950s.

▶ Trams on two lines now closed: Victorian Railways No 43 waits in Barkly Street, Elwood, while No 677 of the Melbourne and Metropolitan Tramways Board heads east along Glenhuntly Road from Point Ormond.

JEREMY WAINWRIGHT

MISHAPS

Operating in busy streets, Melbourne's trams inevitably have their share of mishaps. Because of their relatively low speed, few accidents are serious and some even have an element of entertainment. The year 1953 seems to have been jinxed for Melbourne's trams, as these two pictures show.

DEFECTIVE TRAM NOT TO BE RUN REFER DEPOT STARTER

▶ These two trams collided at the corner of Power Street and Riversdale Road, surprisingly without causing any injuries. The tram bound for Hawthorn, which tipped over at 45 degrees, was empty while the Burwood tram was fully loaded. An unconvincing explanation offered by tramway men was that 'passengers escaped injury because they were packed so tightly they could not be thrown to the floor'. The driver of a following tram said that 'the empty tram was heaved into the air and tilted on its side, as though plucked into the air by invisible fingers'.

▶ Rule number one: Never try to overtake a tram on the right-hand side. This motorist came to grief when his car jammed between two trams in Cotham Road, Kew. Although the two occupants of the car were trapped for 20 minutes while tramway staff, police and civilians levered a door from the car with crowbars to free them, the tramway employee, at the right of the picture, did not seem to find the situation too distressing.

THE SUN

THE ARGUS

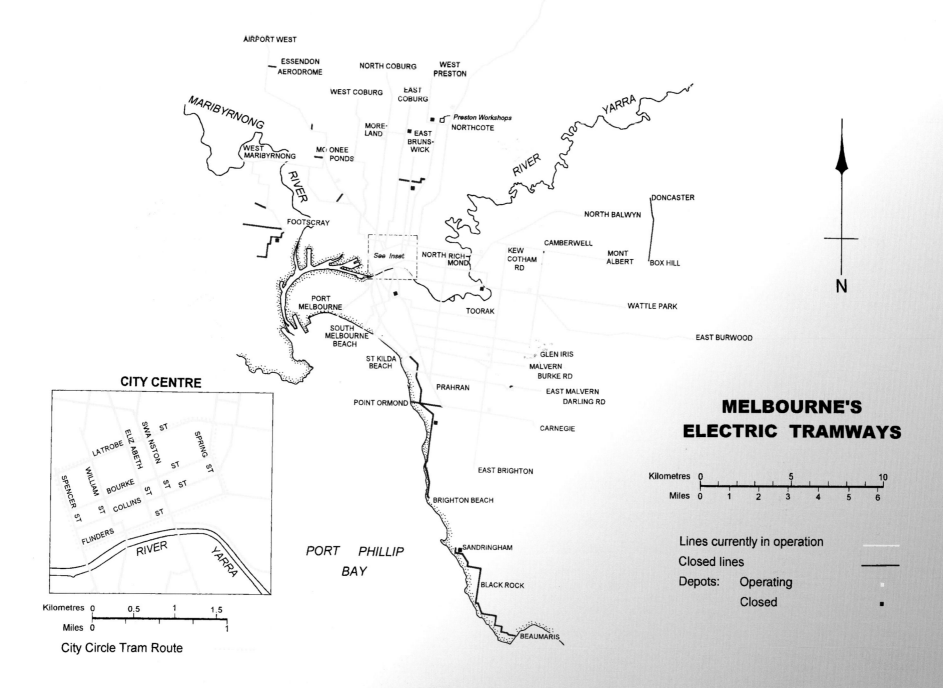

MELBOURNE'S ELECTRIC TRAMWAYS

BUNDOORA R.M.I.T.

AIRPORT WEST

ESSENDON AERODROME

NORTH COBURG

WEST PRESTON

WEST COBURG

EAST COBURG

MARIBYRNONG

YARRA

MORE-LAND

Preston Workshops
NORTHCOTE

WEST MARIBYRNONG

MOONEE PONDS

EAST BRUNS-WICK

RIVER

RIVER

DONCASTER

NORTH BALWYN

FOOTSCRAY

CAMBERWELL

See Inset

NORTH RICH-MOND

KEW COTHAM RD

MONT ALBERT

BOX HILL

PORT MELBOURNE

TOORAK

WATTLE PARK

SOUTH MELBOURNE BEACH

EAST BURWOOD

ST KILDA BEACH

GLEN IRIS

MALVERN BURKE RD

PRAHRAN

EAST MALVERN DARLING RD

POINT ORMOND

CARNEGIE

EAST BRIGHTON

BRIGHTON BEACH

SANDRINGHAM

BLACK ROCK

BEAUMARIS

PORT PHILLIP BAY

N

Kilometres 0 _____ 5 _____ 10
Miles 0 1 2 3 4 5 6

Lines currently in operation _____
Closed lines _____
Depots: Operating ▫
         Closed ▪

CITY CENTRE

LATROBE

SWANSTON ST

ELIZABETH

SPRING ST

ST

WILLIAM

BOURKE

ST

ST

SPENCER ST

COLLINS

ST

ST

FLINDERS

RIVER

YARRA

Kilometres 0   0.5   1   1.5
Miles 0   1

City Circle Tram Route

GONE TO GREENER PASTURES

The Tramway Museum Society of Victoria's trams run on a section of former railway line through open countryside near Bylands. A W1 class tram gives its passengers a breezy ride as it rolls along the Museum's track.

What happens to Melbourne's trams when they finish their useful lives?

The answer used to be, in many cases, that they went on to new careers in Victoria's major provincial cities. Geelong, Ballarat and Bendigo all had tramway systems, operated by the State Electricity Commission. Virtually all of the trams used on these networks were second-hand vehicles from Melbourne.

Trams in these three cities were all replaced by buses. In Geelong the last service finished in 1956, with final closures occurring in Ballarat in 1971 and in Bendigo in 1972. However, in both Ballarat and Bendigo parts of the tram systems have been retained for museum or tourist operations.

Of course, not all of Melbourne's retired trams went to the provincial cities. Many were stripped of their wheels, motors and other electrical equipment, and sold for use as sheds, while others were simply scrapped.

In the 1970s the advent of the Z-series trams led to the disposal of large numbers of early W-series trams. Although old, they were serviceable, and a market developed for their sale in complete condition and ready for further operation.

Many W-series trams were made available to museums in Australia and overseas, while others were sold for use on new tram systems in the USA. Today, trams from Melbourne are in daily service in locations as diverse as Seattle and Memphis. One is in England, bought by Elton John for his garden. After a change of policy in 1990 the disposal of retired trams ceased and they are now retained in storage indefinitely.

Melbourne has its own tram museum, operated by the Tramway Museum Society of Victoria at Bylands, near Kilmore, 65 km north of Melbourne. A number of historic trams are retained in Melbourne itself. These are depicted in the 'Historic Fleet' section of this book.

▲ The city of Christchurch, New Zealand, opened a new tourist tramway in February 1995. Trams run on a circular route around the city centre, and so popular has been the service that an approach was made for an ex-Melbourne tram to provide extra capacity. A retired W-series tram was overhauled and shipped to Christchurch. It is seen here on its first day in its new role in January 1996.

▲ Far from the Melbourne suburbs where it began its career, a tram passes through Ironbark Gully on its way from Bendigo to the outlying suburb of Eaglehawk.

▼ Beautifully restored by the Ballarat Tramway Preservation Society, tram No 26 poses for its portrait on the section of Ballarat's tramways, now operated as a museum line. This is how No 26 looked when it entered service in Ballarat in 1930, little different from its original appearance when built for the Hawthorn Tramways Trust in 1916.

◀ No 44 of the Prahran and Malvern Tramways Trust (restored to its original appearance in Bendigo) in a setting reminiscent of suburban Melbourne around the time of the First World War.

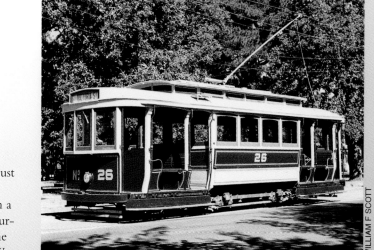

RAY MARSH

▲ Four trams built in 1912 for the Prahran and Malvern Tramways Trust were sold in 1927 to Adelaide, where they continued to run until 1958. One of these unusual trams, No 192, now runs at Adelaide's Tramway Museum.

▲ The tradition of retired Melbourne trams having new leases of life in the provincial cities has continued, with the tourist and museum lines in Bendigo and Ballarat both receiving W-series trams from Melbourne in recent years. One such tram is seen from the verandah of Bendigo's Shamrock Hotel.

▶ Shamrock Hotel provides a handsome background for a tram in Pall Mall, Bendigo. Built in 1914 for the Prahran and Malvern Tramways Trust, it was brought by the State Electricity Commission for use in Bendigo in 1951. A tourist service operated by the Bendigo Trust still runs on this section of track.

RANDALL WILSON

86

IAN HAMMOND

▲ Trams from the Adelaide Museum are occasionally transferred to the city's sole remaining tram line, which links the centre of the city with Glenelg. The 50th anniversary of the conversion of this route from a steam railway to an electric tramway occurred in 1979. A former Melbourne W-series tram is greeted by a large crowd as it arrives at Glenelg during the anniversary celebrations.

BRYAN BECHTOLD

▲ Many thousands of kilometres from home, this former Melbourne tram is still well used as it carries football fans to a game at Mile High Stadium, west of Denver, Colorado. The centre section of the tram has been rebuilt, and in the absence of an overhead power supply, it is powered by a generator on a small trailing vehicle. Some fifteen W-series trams are currently operating in seven cities in the USA.

MELBOURNE'S MOODS

▲ Mist from the nearby Yarra River envelops a tram in Batman Avenue on a cold winter's morning.

◀ Tram drivers brave enough to speed through floodwater can create an impressive bow wave. Nicholson Street is the setting for this picture, taken after a brief but heavy shower.

◀◀ ▲▲ (and above left) Trams can run through water only a few centimetres over the tracks before risking damage to their electrical equipment. A torrential downpour in February 1972 led to these trams being banked up in the area now occupied by the Bourke Street Mall. The situation soon deteriorated into a flash flood, with the trams marooned and a panel van well afloat. Efforts to resume normal services led to chaotic scenes at locations such as Princes Bridge.

MOVING PEOPLE

In 1955, the year in which this article was published, the first stage of the conversion of the Bourke Street lines to electric trams was achieved. These routes had been operated by cable trams until 1940, then by buses.

THE FOLLOWING ARTICLE IS BY MAJOR-GENERAL R J H RISSON, CHAIRMAN OF THE MELBOURNE AND METROPOLITAN TRAMWAYS BOARD

IT APPEARED IN THE AUGUST 1955 ISSUE OF THE JOURNAL OF THE INSTITUTE OF TRANSPORT (AUSTRALIAN SECTION). IT IS THE TEXT OF AN ADDRESS TO THE VICTORIAN BRANCH OF THE INSTITUTE, AND HAS BEEN SLIGHTLY EDITED FOR REPUBLICATION.

Someone, Kipling, I believe, once wrote, 'Transportation is Civilisation'. It is of one element of that civilisation that I am privileged to speak to you this afternoon.

The earliest urban public transport vehicle was possibly the sedan chair, two-man power, or maybe the Venetian gondola, one-man power. The principle of the wheel was known then, but some city streets were not suitable for it – still true, it is said.

There was recently published in the press a summary of sedan chair charges in old London. My recollection is that the fare was several shillings for a few hundred yards. I mention that to quiet for all time carping criticism of modern Melbourne's more modest fares.

I said 'Transportation is Civilisation'. Certainly I have read, and believe, it was the tramcar that made possible and laid the foundation of modern urban development – if you will agree that that betokens civilisation.

▶ Surrounded by vintage motor vehicles in High Street Northcote, a track-cleaning tram heads for the new depot at East Preston with a brand-new W-series tram following behind. Only the outbound track has been laid, with work on the inbound line not yet started.

▶ 1957 saw the end of 'all-night' services, operated by veteran trams such as this example at Brunswick Depot. All-night trams were run by one person, many years before driver-only operation became wide-spread. Four-wheel trams last carried passengers, by day or night, on the Footscray lines, closed in 1962. A handful are retained for track maintenance duties.

B A SILCOVE

NOEL REED

90

The final batch of W series trams was built in 1955–56 for use on new lines running along Bourke Street to East Preston and East Brunswick. The new trams were run in on route 69, from St Kilda to Kew, to ensure they were fully fit to take up their new duties. In January 1956, two brand new trams pass on the level crossing at Kooyong.

Prior to about 1880, cities of western civilisation were limited in size to the radius of horse buses. Now they have no known limit – or had none in the pre-atomic age. Whatever our views on the desirability of gargantuan metropolises (and I for one think it a great pity that three millions of nine million Australians live in two cities), cities of even much more modest size could not exist, as they do, with homes, by choice or of necessity, at a distance from work places, were it not for trams, buses, trolleybuses and today's electric trains. The accent is, must be, on public transport, designed for mass movement of people.

There is, or has been a disposition to refer to some transport authorities as tram-mined, bus-minded, or as the case may be, meaning unreasonably prejudiced in favour of one type of vehicle. That, of course, is foolish. No operator founds his business on prejudice — even, let me assure you, a monopolist operator. Decisions are based on hard facts — economic facts.

That different cities reach different conclusions is not unnatural. It is because their conditions are different. To take a simple case in point. Hobart and Launceston in Tasmania buy electric energy at about 40 per cent of Melbourne's price. (Cheap hydro-electric power is the

reason for that, of course.) They favour trolleybuses, rightly, no doubt, whereas cities of similar size in Victoria might well, and equally rightly, prefer diesel buses.

Let me put in here with emphasis: London is very different from Melbourne. I need not elaborate.

It is safe to say that every city of consequence today has a requirement for some motor buses — for cross-town routes, feeder services, developmental routes, and as a flexible reserve. What to use for other purposes (the normal, basic services of the city system) is more of a problem — trams, motor buses, trolley-buses, or a combination of two or all three of them.

R S JONES

▲ The 1960s saw major infrastructure improvements on the tramway network, but no new trams. Most services were still provided by trams dating from the 1920s. One such tram, No 567, is seen here turning onto new track in Nolan Street, which became Southbank Boulevard when the line was diverted from City Road in 1970 to allow expansion of the Arts Centre.

Melbourne uses trams (767) and buses (300). It will probably add trolleybuses in the future, but not early.

Where to use trams and where buses, is determined by the economics of individual cases. Automatically, the deciding factor is normally density of loading. There is no doubt that on Melbourne's more heavily loaded routes trams remain the most efficient vehicle, both financially and on the score of moving people quickly. Other, lightly loaded routes, are, equally without doubt, bus propositions. Between the two are the less certain cases that must be determined on their individual merits.

The most important factors are these.

FIRSTLY, ROAD COSTS:

Roads built and maintained by the tramway authority (which, incidentally, also pays rates on the space it occupies in the streets for that privilege). Including the necessary overhead system (not excluding substations) they cost today approximately £120,000 per mile of double track in concrete, or £100,000 in ballast.

Against these road and way costs, buses pay only the equivalent of normal registration fees. Municipalities must provide their roads.

Fortunately, nearly all of Melbourne's present tramways were built at a fraction of today's costs. And those tracks are going to be used for many years yet. Were they to be built today, the story would be different.

SECONDLY, ROLLING STOCK:

Trams now cost £10,000 each; buses, £6,500.

The nominal life of a tram is 25 years; of a bus, 8 years. Each is sometimes run appreciably more than its nominal life, but the ratio remains the same.

Like its tram tracks, but to a somewhat less degree, Melbourne's tramcars were built very much below

JIM SELETTO

◀ With their last services run, little future lies ahead for the Footscray fleet of trams following closure of the system on the evening of 11 March 1962.

today's costs. Like the tracks, they will continue in service for many years yet. Most of its buses are relatively new, purchased at modern prices – and still will be worn out before the bulk of the trams.

THIRDLY, RELIABILITY:
Per 100,000 miles, tram 'pull-ins' (breakdowns in service requiring withdrawal of the vehicle and replacement by another) are 22; bus 98: a ratio of 1 to 41/2

FOURTHLY, POWER:
Trams use electric power at approximately 6d. per tram-mile; buses, diesel fuel at a little over 31/2d per bus mile.

FIFTHLY, PLATFORM LABOUR COST:
Nominal, average-maximum, tram capacity is 90 passengers; bus, 60. Most buses have two-man crews, the same as trams. Direct platform labour cost per passenger, therefore, is of the order of 50 per cent higher on buses than on trams. There is the real rub, particularly when I add that wages and salaries, sick pay, retiring gratuities and the like (in short, payments to personnel) make up 70 per cent of the Tramways Board's outgoings.

It will be obvious that some of the factors I have put before you favour trams; others, buses. Each close case must be examined on its merits, and it is apparent that, broadly, the issue is determined by whether or not the density of loading is adequate to warrant the greater capital cost of a tramway, of which the operating cost per passenger is less than that of a bus route.

Where traffic is really heavy, there is another factor. Trams will lift up to 13,500 passengers per hour in each direction; trolleybuses about 10,000; the largest motor buses somewhat less.

In Swanston Street, for instance, the rate of passenger movement reaches 12,000 or upwards per hour, although not for a full hour. It is beyond the accepted capacity of motor buses or trolleybuses.

TRAFFIC CONGESTION
Among the most serious problems besetting transport operators, and their passengers, is traffic congestion in principal streets. Though less acute in Australia than overseas, it is still intolerably serious.

Public transport is not the only sufferer, of course: private transport suffers too. But public transport delays affect many times more people than do delays of private traffic, even though they are represented by a mere fraction of the number of vehicles.

The title of my talk today, 'Moving People' was chosen deliberately. It is not original. I owe it to the General Electric Company of America, which a few years ago produced an excellent educational film with that title of 'Moving People', to emphasise that the basic traffic problem is moving people, or goods, and not, as commonly and erroneously supposed, moving vehicles. It is easy, too, for the average man to look at the obvious foreground of vehicles and assume that there is the essence of the matter – just as it is proverbially easy to fail to see the wood from the trees.

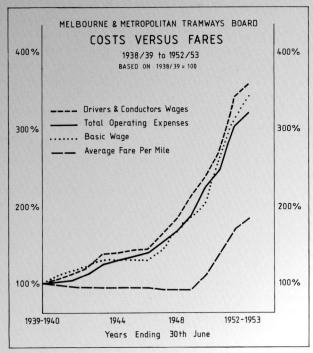

Figure 1

To make my point, as briefly as I can, a traffic count taken by the Town and Country Planning Board in 1947 showed that in the heaviest half-hour of the peak Swanston Street trams carried 5,472 southbound passengers over Princes Bridge on one track, while in the same half-hour two lanes of motor cars and taxis carried 727 people, including the drivers. If you will trust my arithmetic, that means 88 per cent of the total on trams in one traffic lane against 12 per cent in cars and taxis in two traffic lanes.

There were probably a few private buses not counted in those figures. Allowing for them, it appears that the trams carried some 85 per cent of the total in one lane against some 15 per cent carried in the other two lanes.

Those figures were checked again in 1951 and found practically unchanged. You will agree that there has been little change since.

IAN COOPER

▲ Improvements to the tramway system in the post-Second World War years included the provision of double track on the few sections of route which previously had only a single line. This program was not completed until 1989, with the duplication of the outer section of the Carnegie route. Seen near the terminus before this work was undertaken, this tram provided little impediment to cars, but its operation would have been somewhat hazardous after dark.

This is the Town and Country Planning Board's comment in its Annual Report:

> At this time of the day Princes Bridge would be regarded as operating at its maximum capacity . . . For every 10 feet of road space occupied, therefore, 36 passengers were conveyed out of the city in private motor cars, as against 547 passengers in tram cars.
>
> It is therefore apparent that public transport is by far the most economical user of street space when considered in relation to the number of passengers for which it caters.
>
> The public transport vehicle is not the cause of congestion: it is the victim of it.

COSTS AND FARES

If someone says, 'I will be quite happy to travel by public transport if you will guarantee me room and comfort', my reply is, 'Certainly, if you will pay for it'.

Public resistance to realistic fares is astonishing when contrasted with ready acceptance of prices commensurate with costs of goods and services in general.

Melbourne's average fare per mile today is 1.84 times what it was in 1939. The average fare paid per passenger – slightly different – is 2.08 times. Operating costs are approximately 3.25 times!

Figure 1 shows how they have moved. It is based on 1939 figures as 100 per cent. The bottom line is fares. They were constant from 1939 to 1949: in fact, they remained unchanged from 1926 to 1949. Since then, based on average fare per mile, they have risen 84 per cent.

Other lines show the basic wage per hour, now up 250 per cent; drivers' and conductors' wages per mile, slightly higher; and the operating cost per mile, up approximately 225 per cent, or 3.25 times what it was.

In 1951, one of Melbourne's suburban city councils issued to its ratepayers a pamphlet entitled 'Why does my road cost so much?' It showed how costs had risen from 1939 to 1951. These are some of the figures:

Earthwork excavation had gone up by 528 per cent – that means it was costing 6.25 times as much in 1951 as in 1939. Metal screenings had gone up by 242 per cent; sand 362 per cent; cement 108 per cent; bitumen 198 per cent; motor cartage 252 per cent; draw cartage 262 per cent; concrete channels 266 per cent.

In other words, costs were from more than double to more than six times what they had been in 1939.

That was in 1951. I do not know how much they have gone up since, but in the meantime, I remind you, the basic wage has gone up about 30 per cent.

The older ones among you will agree with me that you bought a better suit for 8 guineas in 1939 than you can buy for 30 odd guineas today. I need not remind

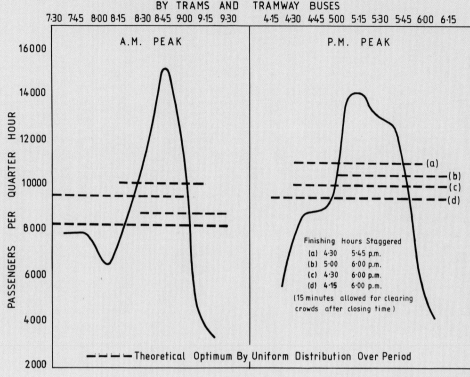

Figure 2

married men of what their wives tell them about the costs of groceries, meat, etc.

Far from being exorbitant in price, public transport is probably the cheapest thing you can buy in this community today.

Getting the bulk of the travelling public, or even if we got all of them, to travel on public vehicles, is not a complete solution of the traffic difficulty, or, should I say, the transportation problem. Large cities the world over, and particularly highly industrialised cities, all face the problem that the great bulk of travelling public require to travel in the same brief periods, going to their work in the morning and returning home from it in the afternoon. All such cities have intense crowd-

ing in those brief peak periods and relatively light traffic in off-peak periods.

It is in peak periods that street congestion is at its worst, and it is the peak periods that impose the greatest strain on transport undertakings. Those undertakings are obliged to provide rolling stock and other capital equipment, and to employ labour to carry the peak traffic, which they do not require for the greater part of the day – but they must meet interest and depreciation, sinking fund and such like charges on the equipment, and often, in addition, pay the labour when they have no use for it.

Naturally, in the interests of economy, which means in the interests of the public who pay for a service, they make constant efforts to reduce the disparity between peak-hour and off-peak demands. The acuteness of this problem varies considerably between county and country and even between city and city in the same country, owing to local conditions. It is, I regret, particularly acute in Australian cities.

Figure 2 shows more eloquently than figures how loading on Melbourne's trams and tramway buses fluctuates over the peak periods mornings and afternoons. It shows numbers of passengers reaching or leaving the central city area per one-quarter hour.

Looking at the am peak, you will see that from 7.30 to 8 am the number remains more or less constant, at a little under 8,000 per quarter hour. They are factory workers. Then from 8.00 to 8.15 am it drops to 6,500. Then it begins to climb, and climb steeply, until, with the white-collar workers reaching the city just before 9 am, it attains for a brief – a very brief – period a rate in excess of 15,000 per quarter hour.

As those white-collar workers go through the front doors and punch the clocks the graph tumbles downwards nearly off the paper. From 9.15 to 9.30 am the average is below 3,500 per quarter hour – a drop of 75 per cent in less than half an hour.

Obviously, the transport authority's task would be much easier, its costs (and therefore the cost to the community) much less, and the comfort of the travelling public would be greatly enhanced, if this high peak could be 'dozed off' into the deep valleys on either side of it.

Until recently, suggestions of staggering have generally been ill-received in Melbourne, and doubtless in most other places. This reception is based not really on merits, but primarily on habit, prejudice, conservatism – general reluctance to accept change and depart from established practice. The great majority of workers of all grades would really benefit from a measure of staggering, and their employers, be their businesses great or small, would not suffer. Shopping, for example, and transaction of much business, would be greatly facilitated.

Thanks to the efforts of certain public-spirited men, particularly the Employers' Federation, we have hopes of some success in this direction in the future.

There is even now a certain amount of staggering of hours in Melbourne, although only a fraction of what is desirable. At Fishermens Bend, for example, starting times are staggered from 7.15 to 9 am. In consequence, the Tramways Board's buses serving Fishermens Bend are able to make, some 5 trips, some 4, and so on; and 49 buses suffice in the mornings, 55 in the afternoons, whereas, if there were no staggering, 133 would be necessary.

We are very grateful for that staggering. We would like the same elsewhere. It illustrates the advantages to be gained by staggering, both on the score of costs and on the score of comfort, for I can assure you that if the workmen travelling to Fishermens Bend had all to be taken at the same starting time they would necessarily travel in much less comfort than they do now.

As it is, in the morning at any rate, I should say they travel in much greater comfort than any other great body of our going-to-work bus passengers.

I have given a somewhat discursive story of the salient points that engage the attention of a public transport operator. If I seem to have devoted myself primarily to our problems, please do not imagine that that is in any sense in complaint. I have done so because telling you our problems has seemed the most direct and expeditious way of offering you some insight into our industry. If there were no troubles, of course, there would be no need for us who direct it, and that would be calamitous.

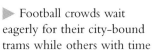 Football crowds wait eagerly for their city-bound trams while others with time to spare stroll westward along Wellington Parade towards Flinders Street.